DATE DUE

BEHIND THE CAMERA

James Cameron

Ron Howard

Spike Lee

George Lucas

Rob Reiner

Steven Spielberg

Ron Howard

Hal Marcovitz

Chelsea House Publishers
Philadelphia

Frontis piece: Ron Howard has been involved with show business all his life. He's one of the few child stars to have successfully maintained a career in Hollywood well into his adult years, even going from acting to directing, where he has enjoyed even greater success and achievement.

CHELSEA HOUSE PUBLISHERS

EDITOR IN CHIEF Sally Cheney
DIRECTOR OF PRODUCTION Kim Shinners
CREATIVE MANAGER Takeshi Takahashi
MANUFACTURING MANAGER Diann Grasse

STAFF FOR RON HOWARD

ASSOCIATE EDITOR Ben Kim
PRODUCTION ASSISTANT Jaimie Winkler
PICTURE RESEARCHER Sarah Bloom
SERIES AND COVER DESIGNER Takeshi Takahashi
LAYOUT 21st Century Publishing and Communications, Inc.

http://www.chelseahouse.com

First Printing

1 3 5 7 9 8 6 4 2

Library of Congress Cataloging-in-Publication Data

Marcovitz, Hal.
  Ron Howard / Hal Marcovitz.
    p. cm. — (Behind the camera)
Summary: A detailed biography of Ron Howard, whose acting career
began when he was just two years old, grew into television and film
success, and led to superstardom as a director of feature films.
Includes bibliographical references and index.
Summary: Aboard the vomit comet — From Opie to Richie — Grand
theft auto — The kid is OK — Pushing the envelope — Great
storytelling —This is the Grinch.
  ISBN 0-7910-6716-5
  1. Howard, Ron—Juvenile literature. 2. Motion picture producers
and directors—United States—Biography—Juvenile literature. 3.
Actors—United States—Biography—Juvenile literature. [1. Howard,
Ron. 2. Motion picture producers and directors. 3. Actors and
actresses.] I. Title. II. Series.
  PN1998.3.H689 M37 2002
  791.43'0233'092—dc21
                        2002002083

Table of Contents

When the Apollo 13 rocket launched in 1970, nobody could predict the struggles that lay ahead for the crew. In directing the film *Apollo 13*, Ron Howard used the facts from the problem-plagued mission to create a gripping story of the astronauts' determination and survival.

Chapter 1

Aboard the Vomit Comet

DIRECTING A FILM about the U.S. space program would be challenge enough for most movie directors. Sticking to the facts of one of America's most famous missions into space offers an even higher degree of difficulty. Throw in a desire to film the scenes in space in true weightlessness, and the end result is a film that maybe only Ron Howard could have pulled off.

Apollo 13, which was filmed in 1994, tells the story of America's ill-fated third mission to the moon in 1970. After the triumphs of the first two moon landings, Apollo 13 was soaring through space when an explosion aboard the craft forced the astronauts to abort the mission and limp home as the ship's oxygen supply and electric power slowly ran out.

The film offered unique challenges, not just to Howard, but to everyone involved. Tom Hanks is one of America's most gifted and accomplished actors. His performance as a lawyer dying of AIDS in the film *Philadelphia* won the Academy Award for Best Actor in 1993. A year later, he won another Oscar playing the mentally-challenged, yet good-hearted protagonist in *Forrest Gump*. But nothing in Hanks' career prepared him for the rigors and challenges of his role as astronaut Jim Lovell in the film *Apollo 13*.

Ron Howard, the film's director, said: "When a director initially considers doing a movie like *Apollo 13*, the first thought is often, 'Well, we might have to crank it up a bit. We'll *base* it on what really happened, but we'll Hollywoodize it.' What really happened in Apollo 13, however, was so suspenseful and entertaining and fresh, it required no Hollywoodizing. As a storyteller, I found that what differentiated *Apollo 13* from a science fiction movie or a cop movie or most other movies was that if you were trying to determine which direction to take your plot, you didn't have to agonize very much; all you had to do was fall back on historical fact."

For Hanks and the other actors in the film, Howard's commitment to the facts meant playing their roles on a movie set unlike any other that had been constructed in more than a century of American filmmaking. Howard decided that since the Apollo 13 astronauts had lived in a weightless environment during their six days in space,

Howard in front of a promotional poster for *Apollo 13*. Directing the true story of the Apollo 13 mission required no "Hollywoodizing," according to Howard, as the actual events were more than exciting enough.

to truly capture the look and feel of space flight on film the scenes aboard the spacecraft would be shot as the actors floated through air. Indeed, Howard wanted no hidden wires or computer-enhanced photography to simulate weightlessness—in *Apollo 13,* the actors would be weightless.

Of course, the question was how to simulate weightlessness without actually going into space. To solve that dilemma, Howard turned to the National Aeronautics and Space Administration—the federal agency in the United States in charge of space exploration.

NASA owned a modified Boeing 707 airplane known as the KC-135. The plane was used by the space agency to simulate weightlessness for astronauts in training for flights aboard the Space Shuttle as well as scientists who would need a weightless environment to conduct experiments. The plane was regarded as an important part of astronaut training because while riding aboard the KC-135, most astronauts would for the first time experience the incredible nausea caused by weightlessness that afflicts most people when they first fly in space. In fact, the KC-135 had been nicknamed the "Vomit Comet."

The reason for the astronauts' stomach ailments has never been nailed down by NASA scientists, although they believe the illness may be attributed to an imbalance in the inner ear caused by the sudden change from normal gravity to a weightless environment. Most astronauts get over the ill feeling after a day or two in space. Nevertheless, nearly everyone who has flown in space has reported severe, unpleasant symptoms.

"The blood rushes to your head, and you'd rather crawl into a corner of the shuttle and be left alone. There's cold

To simulate the zero-gravity conditions experienced in actual space flight, Howard filmed some scenes of *Apollo 13* on a specially modified jet airplane, shown here during a NASA astronaut training flight.

sweating, nausea, vomiting," reported Shuttle astronaut Bob Thirsk after returning from space.

On earth, all people, animals, plants, and everything else exist under the force of gravity. Gravity is a force of nature that permits us to live on the surface of the planet.

Airplanes can defy gravity somewhat—their engines and streamlined designs enable them to fly through the atmosphere, but they are not powerful enough to break the force of gravity and continue on into space.

Airplanes are also affected by "drag"—the friction caused when their bodies rub against fast-moving air. Drag slows down airplanes. Rockets that power the Space Shuttle or propelled the earlier NASA missions are powerful enough to overcome drag and boost a spacecraft out of the grip of gravity.

Once in space, drag and gravity are no longer in force. Any object or person inside the spacecraft will float. The condition is known as "Zero G."

The KC-135 simulates Zero G in the earth's atmosphere by flying in curves known as "parabolas." The plane climbs to an altitude of 36,000 feet—about seven miles high—and then plummets into a steep power dive. As it heads toward earth, the KC-135 flies faster than it would drop if it were simply pulled to the planet's surface by the force of gravity. Thus, by flying faster than the pull of gravity, the KC-135 is able to neutralize the force of gravity. Just as astronauts float freely inside a spacecraft, the passengers inside the KC-135 can drift through air, unencumbered by gravity. They are in Zero G.

But the condition does not last for long. The plane has to pull out of its power dive or it will crash into the surface of the earth. Aboard the KC-135, the effect of weightlessness lasts for only 30 seconds at a time—the period it takes to get to the bottom of the parabola. Once the KC-135's pilot pulls out of the dive, gravity immediately returns—and in force. At the bottom of the parabola, the force of the sudden change results in

As shown in this NASA photo, the KC-135 airplane simulates zero-gravity by flying in steeply curving climbs and dives called "parabolas." Because of the nausea that sometimes accompanies these maneuvers, the cast of *Apollo 13* jokingly referred to the KC-135 as the "Vomit Comet."

"Two G"—gravity at twice the normal pull. Instead of floating freely through the KC-135's cabin, passengers must resist against a momentary feeling that their bodies are weighing twice as much as they would on the surface of the earth. For that reason, the interior of the KC-135 is heavily padded.

Normal gravity returns as the plane heads skyward again. And then, at the top of the next parabola, the power dive begins again and the passengers are treated to another 30 seconds of weightlessness. A routine flight of the KC-135 features 40 or more parabolas.

"Most people think a spacecraft moves like the Millennium Falcon as it zooms by the Death Star at light speed to defeat Darth Vader," Hanks said, referring to the fictional spacecraft of the hit movie *Star Wars.*

He added: "We did this film in the real physical universe. It not only gave us more credence as filmmakers and actors, but it should help the movie become more involving for audiences."

Howard won permission from NASA to build a mock-up of the Apollo 13 spacecraft inside the KC-135 and film scenes while the plane roared through its power dives.

"When they gave us that clearance, that was a huge breakthrough," said Howard.

The two main components of the Apollo 13 spacecraft were the command module, named Odyssey, and the lunar module, named Aquarius. The mission called for the crew members, including Lovell, Fred Haise, and Jack Swigert, to ride to the moon in the gumdrop-shaped command module, which was connected nose-to-nose to the spider-like lunar module. But the explosion ruptured the command module's oxygen tanks, forcing the crew to ride home in Aquarius until shortly before re-entry, when Lovell, Haise, and Swigert transferred back into Odyssey for the splashdown.

To recreate the mission, Howard would need mock-ups of Odyssey and Aquarius. He sought the services of Max Ary, head of the Kansas Cosmosphere and Space

Center, a private museum of space artifacts in Hutchinson, Kansas. Ary founded the museum in 1980; today, the facility includes some 150,000 square feet of exhibit space in Hutchinson, a city north of Wichita. Howard and *Apollo 13* producer Brian Grazer were drawn to the Kansas Cosmosphere because the museum was already in possession of many artifacts from the Apollo 13 command module—switches, gauges, knobs, struts, storage cabinets, seats, and other parts. Years after the mission, Ary learned they were sitting in a NASA warehouse and won permission from the space agency to put them on display in the Kansas Cosmosphere. There were, however, no artifacts from the lunar module. After Lovell, Haise, and Swigert transferred back into the command module, Aquarius was sent adrift in space; friction caused the fragile spacecraft to burn up as it re-entered the earth's atmosphere.

But Ary did own the original blueprints for both modules. Certainly, recreating space vehicles that hadn't flown in nearly 25 years was a monumental task. But the job became even more difficult because the mock-ups not only had to be accurate, they had to include hidden access portals, or openings, for the cameras and other movie equipment. In filmmaking, these portals are known as "wildings." Howard instructed Ary he would need 20 wildings in each of the modules.

The job took Ary and his staff at the Kansas Cosmosphere five months; some 45 engineers and craftsmen working 80-hour weeks in Hutchinson were able to deliver mock-ups of Odyssey and Aquarius in time for filming aboard the KC-135.

For about four weeks, Howard and a cast and crew of 11 flew inside the KC-135, filming scenes for *Apollo 13.*

When the movie opened a year later, audiences saw actor Bill Paxton, portraying Haise, squirting orange juice that turned into floating globules in the Zero G environment, while actor Kevin Bacon, who played Swigert, plucked them out of the air with his tongue. Hanks was filmed floating through the tunnel that connects the command and lunar modules.

Bacon, Hanks, and Paxton were called on to play highly dramatic scenes while floating in the Zero G environment. In one of the movie's most intense moments, Lovell realizes that the accident will wipe out his chance to walk on the moon. While bobbing in Zero G, Hanks faces the other two actors and says: "We just lost the moon."

There was no question, though, that filming the scenes for the adventure of Apollo 13 was an adventure in itself. Normally, directors may take hours to set up a shot and won't roll the cameras until they are absolutely sure conditions such as lighting and sound are perfect; in this case, Howard had no control over the parabolas— he could only shoot film in the short periods of weight- lessness created during the power dives.

The cast and crew had to work in often unbearably cold conditions. Because the astronauts aboard Apollo 13 had to conserve electric power, they shut down the heating system aboard the lunar module. To re-create conditions on Aquarius, Howard had the mock-up refrigerated to a temperature of 34 degrees so that the breaths of the actors would form carbon dioxide clouds as they spoke their lines.

Nevertheless, the dialogue spoken by the actors during the weightless scenes had to be re-recorded in a studio months later—the sound recording equipment aboard the

As a director, the challenge for Ron Howard was to depict the cabin and crew of Apollo 13's command and lunar modules in a way that would make the film seem real to audiences. Howard's strict attention to detail helped make the film an overwhelming success.

KC-135 picked up the blasts from the plane's engines.

Most significantly, the actors had to put in performances while riding out the parabolas—enduring the constant strains of Two G, then being prepared to play the scene in the few seconds of weightlessness available.

"There were times when we'd finish shooting a scene, and I had no idea which way I was going to fall," said Hanks. "It's not a sensation you can liken to anything else. It's not floating like Superman but kind of floating like an angel."

And, finally, there was the matter of everyone's stomachs. For the filmmakers, the Vomit Comet was certainly living up to its reputation.

"Well, now, none of us actually spew, to use one of the many phrases for the term," Hanks said, "but we all got—we all at one point or another felt really . . . "

"Horribly," said Bacon. "Oh, yeah. You have to . . . pick one point and just stare at that point." Bacon pointed to the back of Hanks' head. "This is the point, right back here. I know this part of his head so well, because he was right in front of me, and I just—for hours, I was just looking at this one little dot on the back of Tom's head."

But others along for the ride couldn't keep their stomachs under control.

"One of the camera operators threw up all over Bill Paxton at one point," said Howard.

All the effort was worth the trouble. Howard managed to capture some four hours of weightlessness on camera during four weeks of shooting aboard the KC-135.

Apollo 13 proved to be a blockbuster hit, earning more than $172 million at the box office as well as nine Academy Award nominations, including nominations for Best Picture and Best Actor for Hanks. One of the biggest fans of the movie was Dave Scott, commander of the Apollo 15 mission in 1971. Scott was drafted by Howard to serve as technical adviser for the film. It was Scott's job to warn Howard when he came close to

"Hollywoodizing" the story of Apollo 13.

Scott recalled looking over some of the weightless scenes on a video monitor shortly after Howard and the crew returned from a series of KC-135 parabolas.

Said Scott, "I was up there three times, and I can tell you, what I saw on that monitor is what I experienced in space."

Although he had played small roles in several TV shows in the 1950s, most TV audiences first met Ron Howard when he played Andy Griffith's freckle-faced son Opie in the 1960s series *The Andy Griffith Show*.

Chapter 2

From Opie to Richie

BY THE TIME TV producer Sheldon Leonard spotted Ron Howard in a failed pilot, the 5-year-old red-haired boy was already a veteran performer on the stage and screen.

Howard was born on March 1, 1954, in Duncan, Oklahoma. Duncan is a small prairie town in the southern part of the state, but Howard never got to know Duncan. By the time he was two years old, he was on the road with his parents, Rance and Jean, who were actors themselves.

Rance also directed plays, and when Howard was two years old his father found a small part for his son in a production of

The Seven Year Itch he was directing in Baltimore, Maryland. The play tells the story of a married man who develops a wandering eye for the ladies, and includes a minor part for a little boy.

A short time later Rance Howard went to New York to meet with a casting director about an acting job. The director mentioned to Rance that he needed a young boy for a small part in a movie titled *The Journey,* a Cold War drama about a group of travelers aboard a bus driving through communist Eastern Europe. Rance brought his son in to meet the director the next day, and Howard was selected for the role of Billy Rhinelander. Rance, Jean, and their son were soon on a plane to Vienna, Austria, where *The Journey* was filming with movie stars Jason Robards, Yul Brynner, and Deborah Kerr.

There would soon be other parts for "Ronny" Howard, which is how the young actor was now billed in the credits. He appeared in the film *Frontier Woman* and the 1950s TV shows *Dennis the Menace, The Many Loves of Dobie Gillis,* and *The Twilight Zone.* And then he played a role in a pilot with Bert Lahr, a veteran actor known mainly for his role as the Cowardly Lion in the 1939 film *Wizard of Oz.*

A pilot is a TV show that producers film with the idea that it could lead to a series. The pilot is usually broadcast once on a network, and if fans respond by tuning in the network often gives its approval to film the series. In this case, few viewers watched the pilot, and the show was shelved.

But one person who did tune in was producer Sheldon Leonard, who was in the process of casting actors for a TV comedy based on the exploits of a small-town sheriff.

Leonard was the producer of the enormously popular

TV comedy titled *The Danny Thomas Show*. Thomas was a singer and actor who played a New York nightclub entertainer often befuddled by the demands of life with a wife and two small children.

Leonard was developing another comedy to feature the actor and comedian Andy Griffith. Griffith grew up in the small North Carolina town of Mount Airy and had been able to use many of his backwoods experiences to make audiences laugh in his nightclub shows. Leonard decided to base the new show on a town like Mount Airy and feature Griffith as the sheriff of the town, which would be called Mayberry. Instead of filming a pilot, though, Leonard decided to introduce Sheriff Andy Taylor to TV audiences in an episode of *The Danny Thomas Show*.

The show was slated to air in February of 1960. The plot called for Thomas to be stopped for speeding in Mayberry while driving to Miami for a nightclub appearance. Thomas quarrels with Sheriff Taylor and is thrown in jail. Later in the show, the audience is introduced to the sheriff's aunt and small son.

"I wanted 5-year-old Ronny Howard to play Andy's son," Leonard said. "I had seen him in a failed pilot he made with Bert Lahr, and I was not about to let him get away from me. His father, Rance Howard, had misgivings. He had been coerced into letting Ronny do the Bert Lahr pilot, and he had lost sleep over it. He was genuinely concerned, because he didn't want little Ronny to lose his childhood. I told him how we had protected the two children who worked on *The Danny Thomas Show*. They enjoyed coming to the studio. They bicycled and skated around the lot. Licensed teachers held them to the curriculum standards of the finest private schools. Rance Howard agreed to take a chance."

Small-town comedies like *The Andy Griffith Show* saw much success in the 1960s. Here Andy and Ron are seen at the familiar "fishin' hole" featured in each week's opening credits. Ron used his time on the set to learn about the behind-the-scenes work that went into the making of each show.

The Andy Griffith Show premiered on the CBS television network at 9:30 P.M. on October 3, 1960. It proved to be an immediate and long-running success with fans, staying on the air for eight years. Nearly 250 episodes were filmed.

What's more, the show proved to be a trailblazer, introducing American audiences to a down-home style of comedy. CBS soon produced other so-called "rural comedies" featuring backwoods characters living in log cabins, rooming houses, and farmsteads. The era saw the production of such shows as *Petticoat Junction, Green Acres,* and *The Beverly Hillbillies.*

As for *The Andy Griffith Show,* the show featured a group of zany characters providing the comedy around the levelheaded sheriff, who was usually called on by the end of the week's episode to solve a dilemma and get everybody out of a jam. Among the characters were Barney Fife, the rail-thin and hyperactive deputy; Gomer Pyle, the lovable but dim-witted service station attendant; Floyd Lawson, the incessantly boring barber; and Otis Campbell, the town drunk.

Today, alcoholism is a serious social problem that is no laughing matter, but in the early 1960s Otis could be counted on to provide lots of humor. Almost every week, Otis would come staggering into the Mayberry Courthouse where he would let himself into a jail cell so he could sleep off a night of drinking.

Howard played Opie, the young son of the widowed sheriff. Howard's character was often at the center of the week's plot. Some of the early shows featured Opie sneaking a runaway boy into the Taylor household, defending himself against a bully, and befriending a hobo. And even when Opie wasn't the featured player in the week's storyline, he was usually needed for a few scenes. In fact, each week the show opened with a scene of Andy and Opie walking lazily through the woods, fishing poles over their shoulders, as the background music played the show's theme, a whistled ditty titled "The Fishin' Hole."

Through it all, Rance Howard made sure his son received as normal an upbringing as possible. Rance insisted that Ronny attend a public school, and that the shooting schedule left time for homework and Little League.

"Among my peers I was embarrassed to be an actor," Howard recalled of his school days. "It was not something to be talked about. *The Andy Griffith Show* was the number one show in the country, so I always knew there was something I could do that was unusual and that I could function in an adult environment. But I was the butt of a lot of jokes. My character's name, Opie, rhymes with dopey. . . . I'd have to get into fights with people. Fortunately, I could sort of hang in."

On the set, Howard found himself interested in more than just memorizing his lines. The young actor paid close attention to the other details of television production, developing a fascination for the behind-the-scenes work that went into the each week's show.

"I used to really spend a lot of time hanging around with the crew, looking through the camera, turning the wheels, operating the boom mike—making it go in and out," he said. "The crew would get a real kick showing me what they did. It didn't take me long to realize that the director was the person who got to sort of hang out and play with everybody."

Howard's talent as an actor was soon in demand by other producers. In 1962, Howard was cast in the role of Winthrop Paroo in the movie version of the hit Broadway play "The Music Man." The play tells the story of a fast-talking con man who convinces the citizens of River City, Iowa, to buy dozens of musical instruments for their children so he can organize a boys' marching band. But the con man, Harold Hill, knows nothing about music

While playing Winthrop Paroo in the movie version of the hit Broadway play *The Music Man*, Ron developed the acting skills that would soon land him more TV and film roles.

and is interested only in making a quick buck. Howard played the role of the little brother of Marian Paroo, the town librarian and Hill's love interest. As Winthrop, Howard was required to speak his lines with a lisp. "The Music Man," which starred Robert Preston in the role of Harold Hill, proved to be a major hit of 1962, garnering an Academy Award for Best Music Score and a nomination for Best Picture of the Year.

Howard followed his performance in "The Music Man" with a featured role in the 1962 film, *The Courtship of*

Eddie's Father. Howard again found himself playing the son of a widowed father. As precocious Eddie Corbett, Howard slyly maneuvered his father into romantic relationships hoping he would marry again. It was a meaty role, and marked Howard's acceptance by the Hollywood establishment as more than just a child actor. Indeed, 8-year-old Ronny Howard from Duncan, Oklahoma, was now a bona fide movie star.

Meanwhile, Howard returned each year for his role on *The Andy Griffith Show.* As Opie grew older, the plots involving Howard's character changed. In the later years of the show, Opie dated girls, worked at after-school jobs, and organized a rock 'n' roll band.

He stayed with the show until 1968 when Griffith decided to leave the program for other projects. So the producers had the Taylor family written out of the show—Andy got married and accepted a sheriff's job in another town. The producers renamed the show *Mayberry RFD* and made local farmer Sam Jones the main character. *Mayberry RFD* lasted another two years, then went off the air.

As for Howard, he became a hard-working actor, appearing in a number of feature films and TV shows throughout the 1960s. Audiences saw him make appearances in such popular TV shows as *Daniel Boone, The Fugitive, I Spy,* and *The FBI.*

Rance and Jean Howard still insisted their son have as typical a childhood as possible. By now, the Howards had settled in Burbank, a suburb of Los Angeles, California. Ron attended John Burroughs High School in Burbank, where he edited the school newspaper. He found a steady girlfriend—Cheryl Alley, whom he met in English class.

"I was so quiet," Cheryl recalled. "I couldn't talk. I was almost crippled by shyness. I don't know why he stuck with me. I'm just glad I met him. I couldn't get along with anybody else."

At the age of 15, Howard started fooling around with a Super 8 movie camera. Before the development of home video cameras that record sound and images on videotape, amateur photographers used simple movie equipment that shot film. A Super 8 camera recorded images and sound on a spool of film, each frame measuring a mere 8 millimeters from corner to corner.

Howard titled his first movie *Deed of Derring-Do*. It was a western starring Ron and his brother Clint, and its running time spanned a mere three minutes. The plot consisted of two gunfighters staring down each other on a dusty frontier town street. He entered the film in an amateur moviemaking contest sponsored by Kodak, the film manufacturing company, and placed second. Ron Howard, the film director, had scored his first triumph.

"I guess Ron was 14 or 15, and I was 9 or 10," Clint Howard recalled. "He wanted me to be in this film so he could enter the film festival. I said, 'Of course I'll be in your film, big brother, but it's going to cost you 50 percent of your gross.' It [won] second place in the Kodak Film Festival. He got 24 rolls of film and $50. So I got half the film, which I sold back to him, and I got $25 in cash."

As a filmmaker, he had shown a talent years beyond his age. As a teenager, though, he faced some of the typical problems experienced by young people. Jean Howard recalled her son going through a combative stage in which he often disagreed with his parents.

"We couldn't do anything right," she said. "If we wanted to know where he was going, he'd ask, 'Why? Don't you trust me?' And if we didn't ask, he'd say, 'What's the matter? Don't you care?' I was going to pack his bags,

Ron and younger brother Clint Howard both had a great interest in acting and filmmaking. Ron made his first film at age 15, a three-minute western called *Deed of Derring-Do*.

but at 18 he miraculously turned back into the boy we'd always known."

In 1969, TV producer Garry Marshall had an idea for a weekly comedy that would center on life in the 1950s. The show would feature high school kids and their families, and include all the trappings of life in the '50s—sock hops, greased-down hair, leather jackets, hot rods, pony tails, poodle skirts, and plenty of rock 'n' roll music. Marshall cast Howard in the role of Richie Cunningham, one of the central characters. The Cunningham family would live in Milwaukee, Wisconsin, where Tom Miller, a TV executive who helped Marshall plan the show, had grown up in the 1950s. At first, Marshall and Miller named the show *Cool,* but the title didn't go over well with test audiences. So they changed the title to *Happy Days* and filmed a pilot.

Executives at the ABC television network turned down the pilot, thinking that few people living in 1969 would have much interest in the 1950s. The pilot would not air for three years until it was featured as an episode of *Love, American Style,* a weekly ensemble comedy on ABC that had no regular cast. The title for that week's episode was "Love and the Happy Day." After airing it once, ABC retired the pilot to a warehouse shelf.

One person who tuned in to that week's episode of *Love, American Style* was movie director George Lucas, who was casting parts for a feature-length film about one night in a small California town in 1962. Lucas was looking for actors to play the roles of teenagers in the early years of rock 'n' roll. He was immediately sold on Howard for the role of Steve Bolander, a clean-cut, boring, college-bound kid not unlike the character of Richie Cunningham that Howard played in the *Happy Days* pilot.

The film was titled *American Graffiti,* and it would make movie history. The plot was simple, following four friends as they weave in and out of each other's lives while they spend the last night of summer in a small Northern California town. All the actors turned in incandescent performances. Lucas' sharp direction and attention to detail enthralled audiences. Adding a special dose of charm to the film was Lucas' decision to play rock 'n' roll music for every second of the movie.

Audiences flocked to *American Graffiti,* making it one of the cinema's major hits of 1973, earning $115 million at the box office. The film garnered five Academy Award nominations, including a nomination for Best Picture of the Year. What's more, it established George Lucas as one of Hollywood's top directors, giving him enormous clout with studios. Indeed, Lucas' next project would be a science fiction film based on the old Western cliffhanger serials. He titled the film *Star Wars.*

Howard was the lone actor in *American Graffiti* with any recognition among audiences prior to the release of the film. All the other players were virtual unknowns at the time, but *American Graffiti* would launch their careers and make them into international stars. Richard Dreyfuss, who played Steve Bolander's friend Curt, would later win an Academy Award as Best Actor for *The Goodbye Girl.* Others who got their starts in *American Graffiti* were Charles Martin Smith, Cindy Williams, Paul Le Mat, Mackenzie Phillips, Harrison Ford, and Candy Clark.

"It was a liberating experience," Howard recalled of his work on the film. "Being on location. Working all night. It was the first time I didn't have parental supervision. On the nights I wasn't working, I'd go off to San Francisco and try to sneak into clubs. I looked so young I'd always get thrown out. I'd walk in the door and it was like doing a U-turn."

Meanwhile, a hit musical comedy about teenagers living in the 1950s had opened on Broadway. The play featured plenty of rock 'n' roll music and dancing. It was titled *Grease.*

The 1973 hit film *American Graffiti* launched the careers of many young actors. Although Ron was already a recognized face from his TV performances, the 1950s nostalgia film led to his now-famous role as Richie Cunningham on TV's *Happy Days*.

Back in Hollywood, TV executives decided to capitalize on the public's fascination with 1950s nostalgia. At ABC, executives approached Marshall and asked him how quickly he could put together a show about the 50s. Marshall told them there was no need to start from scratch—the pilot for *Happy Days* had been sitting on the shelf since 1969.

"Television is all about money and safety," Marshall said. "The network wouldn't take a risk on my show until they knew it had a good chance of making some money. It took the success of *American Graffiti* coupled with the popularity of the Broadway musical *Grease* for most television executives to finally say, 'Hey, that's a good idea. Let's do the fifties. We're safe.'"

Howard agreed to join the cast as Richie Cunningham. Donny Most and Anson Williams were cast as Richie's friends Ralph and Potsie. Veteran actors Tom Bosley and Marion Ross signed on as Richie's parents, Howard and Marion Cunningham.

The show premiered on January 15, 1974. From the opening seconds, Marshall left little doubt what the show would be about—the theme music he picked for the show was "Rock Around the Clock," the anthem of rock 'n' roll recorded in 1955 by Bill Haley and the Comets.

The show was a hit. Each week, millions of Americans tuned in to watch Richie, Ralph, and Potsie hang around Arnold's Drive-in, where they listened to rock 'n' roll, ate hamburgers served by waitresses on roller skates, and talked about how they would get themselves out of whatever trouble they had managed to fall into that week. All the actors on *Happy Days* became instant stars.

"It was awesome," Howard said. "For a couple of years it was like being in a rock band. We had this young, teen audience. When we'd make an appearance at a mall it wouldn't be unusual for 15,000 to 20,000 people to show up. . . . I was at the height of my visibility. At that point it was difficult to go places. If I went Christmas shopping I had to keep moving. Once I stopped to pay for something, people would start to crowd around. I didn't take it very seriously, but I was glad to be on the wave."

The public may have been in love with Richie, Potsie, and Ralph, but nobody connected with the show expected the popularity and stardom that would be lavished on an actor who had started out playing a minor character on *Happy Days*. His name was Henry Winkler, and he was a struggling stage actor from New York when Marshall cast him for the role of Arthur Fonzarelli, a high school dropout who boarded in the Cunningham home. "Fonzie," as he was called on the show, rode a motorcycle, greased back his hair, wore a leather jacket, and could usually be counted on to beat up the week's bad guy in order to help Richie and his friends out of a jam. In the early shows, Fonzie had very little to do, usually showing up for no more than a scene or two. But as the show's first season progressed, the producers realized that audiences—particularly teenage girls—were in love with "The Fonz."

Soon, Winkler became the real star, helping *Happy Days* stay on top of the ratings for the 10 years of the show's run. As for Howard, he played the good soldier—showing up week after week to appear in the role of Richie. He began doing other acting as well, appearing in several movies, including *The Shootist,* a cowboy film starring John Wayne, and as Huckleberry Finn in a TV adoption of the Mark Twain classic.

There is no question *Happy Days* had a long and successful run, but eventually the producers and writers found themselves struggling to keep the show interesting and funny. So they relied on Fonzie more and more to carry the show, and soon Howard and the other cast members were reading scripts that centered mostly on Winkler, leaving them little to do but play supporting roles.

Henry Winkler's portrayal of "Fonzie" in the hit TV show *Happy Days* helped keep the show successful for 10 years.

"It was someone's idea at the network to change the show to *Fonzie's Happy Days*," Howard recalled. " . . . I understood that there was a role for me on the show as the straight man. Winkler and I talked openly about what was going on. We acted well together and remained good friends. But the network's wanting to change the name of the show was tough for me to take. I felt slighted."

Eventually, the network dropped its plans to rename the show. Howard agreed to remain in the cast, but by now it was 1977. He was 23 years old and ready for a career change. He had briefly attended college, spending four semesters at the University of Southern California in Los Angeles before dropping out. He had also married Cheryl, his high school sweetheart, and bought a house near Los Angeles.

Since the earliest stages of his career, Howard had been fascinated with the job of the director—the person on the movie or TV set responsible for making the production come to life. Howard wanted to direct, and, soon, he would get his chance.

Directing and acting in a film he wrote himself, *Grand Theft Auto*, Ron had learned a lot from working with B-movie director Roger Corman, for whom he worked in the film *Eat My Dust*.

Chapter 3

Grand Theft Auto

THE DIRECTOR HAS been a vital player in motion picture production for as long as there have been motion pictures. Movies have been around for more than century. Although several inventors experimented with ways to capture motion on film, Thomas Edison is credited with developing the movie camera as well as the movie projector. Ironically, Edison was prompted to experiment with movie cameras as a way to bring images to the sound recordings he was able to make on another of his inventions—the phonograph. However, the process of marrying sound to film would not be perfected for several years. In the early years of the industry, all movies were silent.

Nevertheless, between 1891 and 1893 Edison and his assistant, William K.L. Dickson, made a number of short films at Edison's studio in West Orange, New Jersey. The films produced by Edison and Dickson were short, showing dancers, animals, and boxers. But they nevertheless featured most of the ingredients found on a movie set today—cameras, lights, actors, technicians and, of course, a director to tell everybody what to do. Edison usually took on the job of directing the short features.

As equipment grew more sophisticated the movies grew longer and, soon, an industry was born. By the early 1900s, millions of people in America and Europe were going regularly to the movies in grand and elaborate theaters designed specifically for the cinema.

The first great movie director was Edwin S. Porter, who got his start in the business as a projectionist in a theater. In 1903, Porter directed *The Great Train Robbery,* which told the story of armed holdup of a train by desperate outlaws and thus became the first movie to tell an actual story. The final scene of the film, in which an outlaw draws his gun and aims it at the audience, shocked moviegoers of the time. Many people actually jumped out of their seats with fright.

Certainly, there are many creative people involved in the production of a movie. Among them are the screenwriter, who authors the script; the cinematographer, who plans the camera shots; and the actors, who bring the story to life. Other creative people involved in the process are the set and lighting designers, sound engineers, makeup artists, and special effects designers. At the end of each movie the credits list the names of all the professionals and technicians who played roles in the production. Frequently, there are hundreds of names listed.

Sitting at the head of the whole organization is the director, who has overall responsibility for all creative and technical aspects of the production.

Another vital player in the production of the movie is the film's producer, who is responsible for the business end of the movie. The producer seeks financial backing for the production, enlisting studios or private investors for the project, and takes care of many of the other details, such as the advertising and marketing of the film, hiring the professionals and technicians to work on the project, and developing a budget for the production.

Many American films are produced in Hollywood, California, although, certainly, movies can be produced and filmed anywhere. Nevertheless, in America the word "Hollywood" is always associated with the glitter and glamour of the filmmaking business.

Hollywood got its start as the filmmaking capital of the United States in 1911, when East Coast independent film producers headed west to escape thugs who had been sent to rough them up, destroy their equipment, and put them out of business. The thugs were dispatched by an organization known as the Motion Picture Patents Company, which was composed of the nine largest movie companies in the nation. The Patents Company aimed to control the entire filmmaking industry, from production of the movies to ownership of the theaters. The Patents Company even believed its members had exclusive rights to use of the cameras and other movie-making equipment.

So to evade the roughnecks, producers found what they believed was an isolated spot known as Hollywood in some hills near Los Angeles, California. Today, Los Angeles is a thriving metropolis of some 4 million people, but in the early years of the 20th Century Los Angeles was little more than a frontier town. The first independent film producers arrived in 1911. Two of the early independents to begin making movies in Hollywood were Carl Laemmle, whose company would grow into the studio known as Universal Pictures, and William Fox, founder of the 20th Century-Fox film studio.

As for the Patents Company, it was soon out of business. The federal government sued the Patents Company, claiming its control of the film industry amounted to a monopoly, which was in violation of the nation's anti-trust laws. By 1917, the Patents Company had disappeared, and many of its member companies would soon be out of business as well.

In 1977, Howard read a script titled *'Tis the Season* that he wanted to direct. He knew of veteran film producer and director Roger Corman's reputation for giving opportunities to young directors, so he approached Corman and suggested he look over the script. Corman may be best known for his film *Little Shop of Horrors,* which tells the story of a flower shop delivery boy named Seymour who finds that the unusual plant he has been raising has an unquenchable thirst for human blood. The plant also has the ability to talk, and constantly berates Seymour with the order to "Feed me!" Seymour responds by walking the streets of New York's skid row looking for victims for the plant, whom he has named Audrey.

The film is a cult favorite, airing on late-night TV dozens of times over the years as well as in art movie

B-movie director Roger Corman helped Ron Howard get his start as a director. Corman is perhaps most famous for his film *Little Shop of Horrors*, shot in 10 days on a low budget.

theaters where audiences laugh at the film's ridiculous scenario, campy acting, and bargain basement special effects. One of the actors who played a small role in the film was Jack Nicholson, who would go on to become a major Hollywood star.

The film was produced and directed by Corman and it was a typical Corman production as it was shot in a few days on sets left over from another production, using unknown actors whom Corman could hire for very low fees. Indeed, the entire cost of the production was just $30,000—hardly in the same league with the multimillion budgets approved by studios for major releases today.

"I shot between Christmas and New Year's 1959, using the plant shop set for about 80 to 90 percent of the movie," Corman recalled. "I had to shoot so tight in there I couldn't show the street outside. . . . The plant was primitive as special effects go. . . . But it was effective. In fact, this was one of the simplest, least expensive films in history, and yet we got perfectly acceptable performances—in some cases, their best work— from everybody."

By 1977, Corman had become Hollywood's king of the "B movie"—a term filmmakers use for movies that are done quickly and at a low cost. The term originated in the 1930s when it was common for theaters to show "double features"—two movies for the price of one ticket. The main feature was usually a major Hollywood production featuring important stars; the second film on the bill was the B movie. Today, theaters rarely show double features, but the B-movie business has remained a part of the fabric of the film industry with many quick and cheap productions going directly to the videotape rental market.

Many of Hollywood's top directors got their starts heading B movie productions, including several who learned under Roger Corman. Indeed, Corman gave such directors as Francis Ford Coppola, Martin Scorsese,

Peter Bogdanovich, and Jonathan Demme their first opportunities to direct movies.

The project Corman had in mind for Ron was a film titled *Eat My Dust.* The plot centered on teenagers on the run; most of the action scenes would involve fast car chases and a considerable number of crashes. For somebody who had acted in big-budget productions with the likes of John Wayne, Robert Preston, and Yul Brynner, it was hardly the type of film role Howard had accepted in the past. But he never hesitated. With the opportunity to direct looming on the horizon, Howard signed on, agreeing to play the role of Hoover Niebold in the film.

"I worked 10 days on *Dust* while doing *Happy Days* half days," Howard said. "We shot the film over Christmas. When it came out it was one of Roger's biggest to date. Roger saw we had a hit so he asked me to pitch him story ideas. He got a big kick out of them—a sci-fi idea, a hard exploitation cop movie, a character comedy."

Corman rejected them all. Since *Eat My Dust* had been so successful, Corman wanted to stay with the same formula—young people on the run from the law in a story that would feature many car chases and crashes. Corman had already thought of a title for the as-yet unwritten script—*Grand Theft Auto,* a phrase used by police to describe the charge of automobile theft. In *Eat My Dust,* one of the policemen uses that phrase; Corman sent staff members out to ask movie fans waiting in line what they thought of the title. The fans loved it, and Corman resolved to have a script drafted under that title.

Howard sat down with his father and wrote a script for *Grand Theft Auto.* After working out a story line, Howard called Corman and pitched the idea. "After ten minutes, he gave me the green light. We were in preproduction by

Christmas, and on March 2, the day after my birthday, we started shooting."

Ron Howard—the little boy who went fishing with Sheriff Andy Taylor and the teenager who played straight man to Fonzie—was now a Hollywood director.

As promised, Howard cast himself in the lead role of Sam Freeman. Most of the other cast members were friends and family members. He gave roles to his brother, Clint, who had carved out an acting career for himself, as well as his father. Marion Ross, Richie Cunningham's mother on *Happy Days,* also had a part, as did *Happy Days* producer Garry Marshall. Sam's love interest, Paula, was played by actress Nancy Morgan.

The plot called for Paula to be heading for an unwanted marriage to a rich snob, so she steals her father's Rolls Royce and heads for Las Vegas with Sam. Corman gave Howard a budget of $600,000 for the movie, which was spent mostly on staging the film's many car crashes. The filming took just 15 days.

"Thorough preparation, discipline, toughness in editing, rigid about scheduling—that was Roger's way," Ron said. "I still approach complicated sequences the way I went into that first one."

The movie made $15 million at the box office and another $1 million when Corman sold the rights to air the film to a TV network. It was the most money Corman had ever earned for TV rights. Ron Howard, the director, was on his way.

Meanwhile, Ron was still under contract to *Happy Days.* He also signed on to reprise his role as Steven Bolander in a sequel to *American Graffiti* titled *More American Graffiti.* But he was determined to take more directing jobs. His next opportunity surfaced in 1978

In casting *Grand Theft Auto*, Ron gave roles to his brother Clint and friends from *Happy Days* and *American Graffiti*.

when he was offered the job of directing a TV movie for the NBC network titled *Cotton Candy*. It was a story about high school kids in love. Again, Howard invited in familiar faces for the film. Charles Martin Smith from *American Graffiti* was cast in one of the lead roles. Howard also found a role for his brother, wife, and mother. Then he drafted 400 students from Lake Highland High School in Dallas, Texas, for parts

In 1978, Ron directed the TV movie *Cotton Candy*. While still a small production, *Cotton Candy* allowed Howard to develop the directing skills that would serve him well on later projects.

as extras in the film, and shot many of the scenes at the Texas high school.

It was perhaps a step up from the B movie work he had done for Corman, but *Cotton Candy* was still regarded as a minor production—the budget was about $1 million— tiny by Hollywood standards. Still, Ron was delighted with the film and confided that at least for now, he had no desire to take on a more complicated project. "I am better off at this stage of my career trying to make sleepers than to do pictures everyone has high hopes for," Ron said at the time.

As he spent time in Dallas organizing the production, it soon became obvious that as much as he wanted to stay behind the scenes as a director he was still, nevertheless, Richie Cunningham. While eating one night in a restaurant, Howard discovered that a fan had stolen the leftovers from his dinner plate. "I can understand somebody grabbing my hat," he said. "But my chicken bones?"

Directing film legend Bette Davis for the TV
movie *Skyward* was Ron's first big challenge
as a director. After some initial awkwardness,
the 73-year-old Davis and the 26-year-old
Howard got along fine.

The Kid is OK

AFTER DIRECTING A low budget theatrical film for Roger
Corman featuring mostly car crashes, and a bubblegum romance
about teenagers in love, Ron's next directing assignment called
for him to head a production starring one of America's most
respected and talented actresses.

Bette Davis's career in the movies started in the 1930s. She
won Academy Awards in 1935 and 1938, and remained one of
Hollywood's major stars until her death in 1989. In 1980, she
agreed to star in a made-for-TV movie titled *Skyward*. She
played a retired barnstorming stunt pilot who meets a young,

wheelchair-bound girl who dreams of learning how to fly. In the film, Davis's character agrees to teach the handicapped girl to pilot an airplane. Ron Howard joined the production as director.

Although Howard had acted alongside some of Hollywood's biggest stars, he was never in a position to tell them what to do. But now, as the director, he found himself responsible for telling the great Bette Davis how to speak her lines and what type of emotions he expected to see in the various scenes.

He admitted to being overwhelmed by the job ahead. She was, after all, 73. He was just 26. "She used to refer to me as 'Mr. Howard,' a little bit sarcastically," Ron recalled. "And I kept saying, 'Please, Miss Davis, call me Ron.' And she would say, 'I'll call you Mr. Howard until I decide whether or not I like you.'"

In fact, the first day of shooting had plenty of awkward moments. "The first time I went up to give her some direction she acted very startled," Ron said. "And she said, loud enough for the crew to hear, 'What of any consequence could this child possibly have to say to me?' I kind of laughed along with the crew, nervously."

Eventually, Bette Davis decided she liked Howard. By the end of the filming, she had decided to call him "Ron." *Skyward* aired that year on TV. The film served as a valuable milestone in Howard's career because it gave him the opportunity to direct a major film star—particularly a star with decades of experience on the screen.

While filming *Skyward* Howard met Brian Grazer, a Paramount movie studio executive who was serving as executive producer for a number of TV comedies. Both men had offices at the Paramount studio, and both men were anxious to break into theatrical films. Howard and

Grazer started talking over ideas. Grazer had recently clipped a story out of a newspaper about a prostitution ring that operated inside the New York City morgue. Grazer thought the story had a lot of potential as a comedy, and Howard agreed. They formed a partnership and hired screenwriters to develop a script titled *Night Shift*. Grazer would serve as producer and Howard as director. When the script was finished, Grazer started shopping it around to movie studios, seeking financial backing to make the movie. As for Howard, he took on more TV directing jobs while still appearing in *Happy Days* and other TV shows.

By 1981 *Night Shift* was in production. At first, Howard and Grazer tried to recruit comedians John Belushi and Dan Aykroyd for the roles of the morgue workers. The two comics from *Saturday Night Live* were at the height of their popularity and would guarantee an audience for *Night Shift*. But Belushi and Aykroyd had their choice of scripts, and they turned down the project. Instead, Howard and Grazer cast Henry Winkler—Fonzie from *Happy Days*—in the role of Chuck Lumley, the conservative, shy morgue worker who lets himself get talked into the idea of running the prostitution ring. For the role of Bill Blazejowski, the zany character who comes up with the plan, Howard discovered a little-known actor whose gift for physical comedy fit the production perfectly. That actor was Michael Keaton, whose performance in *Night Shift* would catapult him to stardom. In the coming years, Keaton not only proved adept at humor—he would play the title character in the supernatural comedy *Beetlejuice*—but he would also take on challenging dramatic roles, such as the drug- and alcohol-addicted executive in *Clean and Sober*. And Keaton would make his mark as an action

The brainchild of Ron and Paramount executive Brian Grazer, *Night Shift* was a dark comedy about an escort service operated out of a New York City morgue. Ron cast his old friend Henry Winkler for one of the starring roles.

movie hero, starring in the first two films in the enormously popular *Batman* series.

If audiences follow *Night Shift* closely, they'll spot two other familiar faces in minor roles. Kevin Costner, on the way to stardom, appears briefly in a party scene in the movie, speaking a single line. Shannen Doherty, soon to star in the hit TV series *Beverly Hills 90210,* had a minor part as well.

Night Shift was not a major hit—it grossed just $27 million at the box office. But the film made people laugh, critics praised the acting and direction, and it established Howard and Grazer as moviemakers who could deliver a film on time and within budget.

Howard's next directing job was another comedy, but this time the production was far more ambitious. Again, Grazer conceived the idea: a man meets a mermaid, falls in love, and gives up everything for her. Howard and Grazer commissioned a script for the film, which would eventually be titled *Splash.* In the role of Madison the mermaid, Ron cast Darryl Hannah, a dazzling and beautiful actress who had appeared in a number of films, always in supporting roles. The role of Allen Bauer, the befuddled New Yorker who falls for her, was played by Tom Hanks, a young actor who appeared in the TV series *Bosom Buddies* but had done little film work. Comedians John Candy and Eugene Levy were cast to provide the comic relief.

While the writers worked on the script, Howard and Grazer found out that another comedy about a man and a mermaid was also in the planning stages. This film was to star Warren Beatty, one of Hollywood's biggest names. Herb Ross, who headed production on such hits as *Funny Girl, The Turning Point,* and *Goodbye, Mr. Chips,* would direct.

"Warren Beatty was going to be in this other picture," said Lowell Ganz, one of the screenwriters who worked on the *Splash* script. "Herb Ross was going to direct. Monster, monster power project. And then there was us. . . . I'd say, ' . . . *We're the other mermaid movie!'* "

Splash hit the theaters in 1984 and was an immediate blockbuster. The film earned $109 million at the box office. Darryl Hannah and Tom Hanks became big stars and Ron Howard found himself the hottest director in Hollywood. Audiences and critics loved his movies and actors were anxious to work with him.

As for the other mermaid movie, it turned out that Howard and Grazer had nothing to worry about. The film never went into production.

"*Splash* was the turning point," said Howard. "It was Tom Hanks' first major film. Daryl Hannah had been in films but was not a movie star. John Candy had been in some films but hadn't really done a big part. Actors loved *Splash*. They liked the way it established Hanks. I've established two people successfully, Keaton and Hanks. I don't claim credit for Kevin Costner's career. I put him in a party scene in *Night Shift* because I needed someone who could speak a line. Years later I saw him again and asked if I had been nice to him that day. He said yes."

Howard may have had a knack for taking unknowns and making them into stars, but he was also anxious to work with bona fide Hollywood talent. He hadn't worked with a true star since directing Bette Davis in *Skyward* some four years before. He was also anxious to break out of the mold as a director of lighthearted comedies. It was Henry Fonda, the veteran screen actor, who once counseled him to take chances with his career.

"I'm not an adventurous person," says Ron. "But as Hank said, taking risks is important. It's a fine line because you don't want to be suicidal, but it's important to keep testing."

Howard developed an interest in a project that would feature some elements of science fiction and comedy,

Years before *Apollo 13*, Ron directed actor Tom Hanks in the film *Splash* — a comedy about a young man who falls in love with a mermaid. The 1984 release scored a huge hit with fans and boosted the careers of both Howard and Hanks, as well as "mermaid" Darryl Hannah. Here Ron poses with the cast.

but for the most part the film would examine the social consequences of growing old in America. The story was centered in a retirement community in Florida and followed eight people as they wrestled with the realities of approaching death. The film was titled *Cocoon*.

There would be no future stars waiting for their big breaks cast for this movie. To play the roles of the aging retirees, Ron recruited some of Hollywood's most veteran actors. Hume Cronyn, Don Ameche, Jessica Tandy, Maureen Stapleton, Gwen Verdon, Wilford Brimley, Jack Gilford, and Herta Ware all agreed to take roles in the film, which meant they would be taking direction from Ron, who was now a big-time director but was still, in many people's eyes, the kid who played Opie.

Each of those actors had spent a lifetime in entertainment. Cronyn and Tandy, husband and wife, were among America's most respected stage actors. Gilford was an early pioneer of TV comedy and drama. Ameche had been well known to American audiences since the 1930s, and was still recognized for his role as Alexander Graham Bell in a filmed biography of the inventor of the telephone. Maureen Stapleton won an Academy Award in 1981.

The film paints a sad picture of aging in America. Cronyn's character, Joe Finley, is dying of cancer. Ben Luckett, played by Brimley, loses his driver's license when he fails an eye test. Herta Ware, playing Rose Lefkowitz, suffers from Alzheimer's disease; throughout the movie, her memory deteriorates and she finds herself unable to recognize her friends and, eventually even her husband Bernie, who is played by Gilford. In an early scene, Joe Finley, Ben Luckett, and Art Selwyn, played by Ameche, pause briefly in the doorway of a retiree; inside, doctors work frantically to resuscitate the man.

Directing *Cocoon* gave Ron the chance to direct some of Hollywood's golden names—including Don Ameche, Maureen Stapleton, and Jessica Tandy.

After a few seconds, the man's vital signs disappear, and the doctors give up. Finley, Luckett, and Selwyn exchange pained expressions, and move on.

One day, Finley, Luckett, and Selwyn discover some unusual rocks in the bottom of a swimming pool they've been using secretly. After swimming in the pool, the men find a new vigor; what's more, their ailments seem to go away. Even Joe Finley's cancer goes into remission.

It turns out the objects at the bottom of the pool aren't rocks, but cocoons that have been rescued from the sea floor by aliens who departed earth 10,000 years ago. The cocoons contain the slumbering bodies of friends that were left behind. To awaken their friends the aliens have been charging the water with a life-giving force, and that is why the three aging men have been feeling young again.

For the remainder of the movie Finley, Luckett, and Selwyn and their wives wrestle with the question of whether to take advantage of the "Fountain of Youth" to prolong their lives and, later, whether to accompany the aliens to their home planet.

One of the aliens promises them that life on his planet of Antares will be different than the life they have come to know on earth. "I promise you . . .you'll all lead productive lives," he says.

Bernie Lefkowitz elects to stay behind. "Nature dealt us our hand of cards and we played them. Now, at the end of the game you're looking to shuffle the deck," he tells the others.

Luckett replies: "The way nature's been treating us, I don't mind cheating her."

In the movie, Howard relies on the use of symbolism— a technique employed by many directors to send a message to the audience without the use of dialogue. For example, when Rose Lefkowitz dies, Bernie carries her frail and lifeless body to the swimming pool, then immerses her in the water. It is as though he were trying to Baptize her, giving Rose a chance to be "born again"—not in the religious sense, but physically. By now, though, the waters have lost their healing powers and his effort is futile.

An alien named Walter has watched this scene sadly. He tells Bernie: "I've never experienced the pain, the grief associated with death before. I've never had anyone close to me who died."

Another example of symbolism can be found early in the film. When Ben flunks his eye test, he covers his beloved car with an old parachute. It serves the same purpose a shroud would serve in a morgue—to cover a dead body. To Ben, who will never be permitted to drive again, the freedom offered by driving has been lost forever.

And finally, Howard employs symbolism in his portrayal of the aliens—when their true images are finally revealed, they are shown as glowing essences of light in vaguely human forms. An alien named Kitty is played by Tahnee Welch, the beautiful daughter of American sex symbol Raquel Welch. Kitty and the other aliens mingle among people by wearing synthetic human skins. When Kitty peels off her human skin, audiences see the aliens for what they are—bright, beautiful beacons of light. Clearly, it is up to the retirees to follow the beacons to their new lives.

Ben tells his grandson: "Where we're going, we won't be sick, we won't get any older, and we won't ever die."

During the filming, Howard found that he didn't have to worry about Ameche, Cronyn and the other film veterans questioning his judgment, as Bette Davis had done on the set of *Skyward*. Howard said he had Wilford Brimley mostly to thank for that.

"Wilford's a testy guy, not an easy guy to work with all the time," Ron said, "but he has great instincts. Many of his scenes were totally improvised. Wilford set a spontaneous tone, and the other cast members felt challenged by it. They weren't used to working that way but most of them wanted to try it."

Indeed, some of the scenes were so spontaneous that the actors themselves were shocked by their willingness to experiment. In one scene, the couples go dancing at a disco. Art Selwyn, played by Don Ameche, gets so caught up in the excitement of the music that he jumps into a vigorous and athletic break dance. Ameche—76 years old at the time of the filming—insisted on doing the break dance himself.

"Almost all the shots in that scene are me," Ameche said. "We filmed it in a real break dance club in Tampa on the last day of shooting. It was a weird place. You can't believe how people were dressed!"

There is no question that *Cocoon* was a risky project. At the time, the trend among filmmakers was to produce movies aimed at young people. This was the era of the "Brat Pack," the group of young actors and actresses, including Rob Lowe, Ally Sheedy, Mollie Ringwald, and Emelio Estevez, making their marks in such movies as *The Breakfast Club, Sixteen Candles,* and *Fast Times at Ridgemont High.* Would young people care about the problems faced by aging Americans?

The answer was provided when the film was previewed before test audiences. Often, a studio will want to gauge how a film would be received before it gives the final authorization to release the movie to theaters. Many times, depending on how the test audiences react, the film's release may be delayed while changes are made. To perform the tests, ordinary people are hired to sit in theaters to watch special screenings of the films. At the conclusion of the screenings, they are asked to fill out questionnaires or participate in focus groups led by

On *Cocoon*, as on *Skyward*, Ron was the young director faced with earning the respect of older, more experienced actors. The cast warmed up to Howard almost immediately, and the sci-fi/comedy proved a huge hit with audiences.

specialists trained to gauge their impressions of the films they were asked to see.

In the case of *Cocoon,* the test audiences responded enthusiastically.

"Although people like the science fiction and think the effects are good, everyone who fills out the preview cards really loves those characters," Ron said shortly after the previews were completed. "And that cuts across all age groups. We didn't find 17-year-olds saying, 'We love it when the spaceship goes up' and 50-year-olds relating to the old people. *Everybody* is saying, 'Those are great characters. They're really funny.' I find that heartening."

The film turned out to be an even bigger blockbuster than *Splash,* earning more than $112 million at the box office. The critics praised the film as well. *New York Times* film critic Janet Maslin called it "this season's reigning fairy tale." Lawrence O'Toole, film critic for the Canadian news magazine *Maclean's,* said, "Tenderhearted and beautifully structured, the movie has a special lightness of being, and its large cast is uniformly exemplary." In *Time* magazine, critic Richard Corliss wrote, "One hopes that moviegoers will take *Cocoon* to their teenage hearts and make a box-office smash of the summer's sweetest, saddest, most exhilarating fable."

Not only did critics and audiences enjoy *Cocoon,* fellow moviemakers liked it enough to honor the movie. For directing *Cocoon,* Ron was nominated for a Directors Guild of America Directorial Achievement Award—he didn't win, but he took the nomination as recognition that he had earned the respect of his peers.

"It was a real human drama and science fiction that I thought was very tricky. As a young director it was a real challenge. I was so thrilled with the way the performances worked. When the film came together and was popular and successful, and I got my first Director's Guild nomination for that movie I was just very proud of the way it all worked," Ron said. "I really felt like for the first time I genuinely had something. I had made great headway when I chose *Splash,* and all of a sudden I felt that people were still giving me a lot of credibility but I knew that the film needed to confirm in people's minds that I was here to stay. I put a lot of pressure on myself, a lot. I didn't talk about it. I'm embarrassed to say that, but I felt that almost every day. It was a huge relief when *Cocoon* was embraced by critics. I think it meant a lot for my future."

Ron's father Rance had a small part in *Cocoon,* playing a policeman who pursues the retirees and aliens as they rendezvous with the spacecraft. Rance said that as he watched his son work on the set, it was clear that Ron had arrived as a Hollywood director, and would now be a major force in American filmmaking.

He said, "I had gone down and was watching him—he was up on a Chapman crane or something, way up there, and he told Wilford Brimley to come in here, and he said, 'Don, Don Ameche, Don are you OK?' And I thought, 'This kid is a director. The kid is OK. He's made his goal.'"

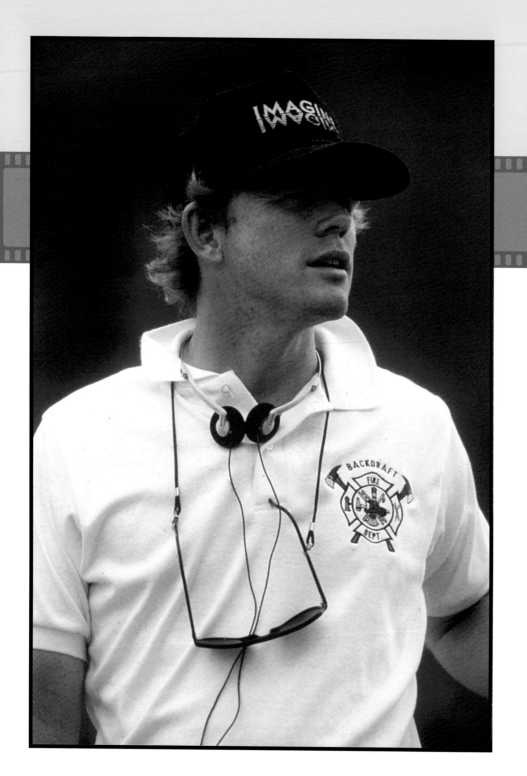

Here's Ron at work on the set of *Backdraft*. The 1991 film followed the lives of Chicago firefighters and combined character-driven plot with spectacular special effects.

Pushing the Envelope

FOLLOWING THE SUCCESS of *Cocoon,* Howard's next project was *Gung Ho,* a film about a Japanese automobile company taking over an American factory. The film, which starred Michael Keaton, was played mostly for laughs, but it did explore some of the hardships of blue-collar workers in America and the culture shock they faced when they suddenly found themselves building cars for new bosses from Japan. The film was a modest success, garnering $51 million at the box office.

During the production of *Gung Ho,* Howard had the opportunity to play the role of Opie Taylor one final time in the TV movie *Return to Mayberry.* The movie revisited the town, checking back with Andy, Barney, and the other characters from the old TV show. Ron saw it as the last time he would act in front of the cameras—with the exception of playing cameo roles from time to time.

After *Gung Ho,* Howard agreed to direct a fantasy film that would be produced by George Lucas. Following *American Graffiti,* Lucas directed the landmark science fiction film *Star Wars,* which established him as one of America's most influential filmmakers. He specialized in science fiction and fantasy, and other directors soon fell in line behind him, making films in the genres of science fiction, fantasy, sword and sorcery, comic book-style adventure, and horror.

To create the images of spaceships streaking through the galaxy, prehistoric monsters chasing adventurers on tropical islands, superheroes flying through the clouds and wraiths materializing from wisps of fog, Lucas established Industrial Light and Magic, a special effects studio near his home in Marin County, California.

Special effects have been a part of filmmaking almost from the start of the industry. It is believed that the first use of special effects was in a short film produced in 1893 by Thomas Edison and William K.L. Dickson titled *The Execution of Mary, Queen of Scots.* As the title suggests, the film dramatized the death of the queen, who lost her head to the executioner's ax in 1587. To create the image of the execution, Edison and Dickson first filmed an actress in costume led to the chopping block by the executioner, then stopped the camera just before the ax was ready to fall. The camera, as well as the actor playing the executioner, remained frozen while the actress was replaced with a mannequin. Once the substitution was made, the camera rolled again. The ax came down, severing the wooden head from the body of the mannequin. The whole scene moved so fast that the audience never noticed the substitution. Many horrified people walked out of the theaters fully believing an actress had been beheaded in the movie.

More often, though, it was easy to tell when the director employed special effects—particularly as movie audiences became savvy about what they were watching. The directors of the 1930s Flash Gordon serials weren't fooling anybody when they filmed live lizards trampling toy spaceships. Certainly, Roger Corman never thought anyone would believe the giant rubber artichoke he devised for *Little Shop of Horrors* was an actual man-eating plant.

By the time George Lucas established Industrial Light and Magic, special effects work on movies had become a sophisticated art utilizing lifelike miniatures, robotics, and computer-generated illusions to create scenes of incredible imagery and to provide false color and other enhancements to the final print of the film.

Willow, a film about medieval-era heroes battling to save the life of a baby princess, contained an abundance of special effects, including 9-inch-tall characters, a two-headed fire-breathing dragon and the transformation of a stone figure into a live bird. "It has lots of sword fights, chases, action, all that stuff," Howard said.

Howard was anxious to direct *Willow* for several reasons. He had worked with special effects on *Cocoon,* but that was, after all, a film about the social consequences of aging in America. Now, Howard wanted to direct a movie in which the special effects would dazzle the audience. He also wanted to work with Lucas.

Ultimately, the film fell flat. It was produced with a budget of some $35 million, and although it earned $73

Howard's medieval fantasy *Willow* used dazzling costumes, make-up, and effects to create a fairytale world of heroes and princesses.

million at the box office the studio expected a lot more out of a collaboration between Ron Howard and George Lucas. Critics panned the film as well.

Roger Ebert, the influential film critic for the *Chicago Sun-Times,* wrote: *"Willow* is a fearsomely ambitious movie, but it is not fearsome, and it is not wondrous, and it is about a journey too far down a road too well-traveled by other movies. It's a fantasy about the quest of a lovable little person and his heroic newfound friend to return a lost baby to where it belongs, and to outsmart a wicked queen and kill a two-headed dragon in the process. In other words, standard stuff."

Ron says now that he knows what went wrong. "It was a great, great collaboration, but halfway through the process I realized that for the first time, I was trying to make somebody else's movie," he admits. "I was trying to get into George Lucas's head because I trusted his tastes and his instincts better than I trusted my own. George is a really fascinating guy to work with in that he really is a gifted non-linear thinker. His problem-solving process is sort of fascinating. He'll be looking at a problem and all of a sudden come up with a solution that is actually way off the track but accomplishes the objective you were searching for. It was pretty inspiring to see the way he worked, and I was fairly happy with the movie when all was said and done. I told myself that when it was over that if I could avoid it, I would try to stay out of that situation; I was going to make movies and rely upon my point of view—certainly collaborate with people, but I wasn't going to commit to a film until I thought I understood it, and could rely upon my instinct."

Two years before, while working on *Gung Ho,* Howard conceived an idea for a film about the trials and troubles of young parents. At the time, his daughter Bryce was four years old and his twin daughters Jocelyn and Page were less than a year old. Howard and his wife Cheryl often found themselves struggling to balance their professional lives with the demands of parenthood.

The film *Parenthood* was released in 1989 to enthusiastic reviews as well as widespread acceptance by the audience. The movie earned $132 million at the box office. Many of the people who flocked to the film seemed to be young

In the movie *Parenthood*, Ron used the talents of comedian Steve Martin to create a warm and honest portrait of the troubles and joys of family life. Here, Steve fills in as the cowboy clown at his son's birthday party.

middle-class parents who empathized fully with the aches and confusion suffered by stars Steve Martin and Mary Steenburgen.

Parenthood contained no special effects—no genies popping out of bottles, no Jedi knights dueling with light sabers, no masked heroes stalking villains through the shadows. It was a movie that concentrated fully on its story and the work of the actors.

Movie critic Desson Howe wrote in *The Washington Post* that *Parenthood* is "punchy entertainment for the open-minded family, the kind that realizes Home Sweet Home is—well, an interesting idea. . . . Most of the time, the punch lines are unobtrusively crafted (and very often, bitingly funny), so you don't feel like a couch potato for laughing; where things are smarmy, the performers revive the dramatic honesty, particularly everyfather Martin, who perseveres through the spiritual brutalities of parenthood" with "mugging tenacity."

In his next project, Ron would tackle a subject rarely dealt with in motion pictures. For decades, Hollywood had made hundreds of movies about policemen but largely neglected firefighters—public servants whose jobs are every bit as dramatic and life-threatening as those of the cops. Indeed, whenever a movie about firemen did make it to the screen, Hollywood never seemed to know how to tell their story. The 1974 film *The Towering Inferno* was certainly a blockbuster, but it hardly gave a true account of the lives of firemen. The film was about the plight of people trapped on the top floor of a burning skyscraper and the efforts made to rescue them. The movie was hardly a true depiction of professional firefighting; it was part of the genre of 1970s "disaster" movies containing huge, special-effects laden productions that featured a lot of havoc, a lot of action, and not much story.

A critically-acclaimed film about firemen that has become a cult favorite is the 1967 movie *Fahrenheit 451,* based on a short story by science fiction writer Ray Bradbury. This movie does not depict the heroics of firemen, either. The film is set in a future totalitarian society where it is forbidden to read books; firemen aren't called on to put out fires, but to arrest book owners and burn their collections. Whenever a fire engine streaks by pedestrians hurry to the scene, not to watch the firemen extinguish a blaze, but to set fire to somebody's books. The title *Fahrenheit 451* refers to the temperature at which paper burns.

But finally, in 1991, Ron Howard guided *Backdraft* onto the screen. The film told the story of brothers Stephen and Brian McCaffrey, who follow their father into the Chicago Fire Department, picking up their story 20 years after his death. There is trouble between the brothers: Stephen is hot-tempered and unpredictable; his wife has left him because he takes too many risks on the job. Brian has drifted into the fire department after failing at other jobs; even now, he isn't sure whether he has the nerve to fight fires. Howard fans who thought they were getting a character-driven story like *Cocoon* and *Parenthood* were not disappointed; but *Backdraft* offered much more—perhaps the most realistic fire scenes ever committed to film.

To help provide the special effects, Howard enlisted Industrial Light and Magic to create the appearance of flames in many of the scenes by using computer-generated images. For example, in one scene two firemen race along a burning rooftop as balls of fire explode around them,

To create realistic fire scenes for the film *Backdraft*, Ron combined computerized special effects with real-life pyrotechnics. The film was a great learning experience for Howard.

causing the building to collapse. "There was absolutely no way to accomplish this scene live; the safety factor made it impossible," said Ron. "It was clearly going to be accomplished as a visual effect. This one is for [Industrial Light and Magic]."

Nevertheless, computer-generated images alone were not going to provide the realism that Ron desired for the film. To truly depict fire in the movie, he wanted to film fire.

"The fire scenes in *Backdraft* were a really unique challenge that taught me some important lessons," said Howard. "I didn't know how we were going to do it; in the beginning I thought it would all be, primarily, special effects. I remember the day when I went to Allen Hall who was heading up the physical effects team and I said we can't do this on the computer. There are two or three huge shots, with a lot of fire, that we can do with miniatures and a little computer-generated stuff and those will be ILM shots, but everything else we're going to have to do physically. It's going to be your ballgame, can you do it? He said, 'Yeah.'"

To star in the film, Howard cast Bill Baldwin as Brian and Kurt Russell as Stephen. For three weeks, Howard, Baldwin, and Russell attended the Chicago Fire Department's academy, participating in actual training courses taught to student firefighters and attending many fires themselves. Also, Howard drafted several Chicago firemen to work as advisors on the set and to appear in scenes themselves. Finally, there was no question that the script would reflect an accurate account of the lives of firefighters—the screenwriter, Gregory Widen, was a former Chicago fireman.

Howard, Hall, and special effects chief Clay Pinney tackled the problem of filming fire in a variety of ways.

Ron had always respected firemen and the hard work they do. In *Backdraft*, he centered on the lives of two brothers who followed in their father's footsteps as Chicago firefighters. Here, star William Baldwin races through a burning doorway.

Pinney designed gas jet burners similar to those found on stoves to deliver flames on demand. The burners were contained in pipes that were built into the sets. Pinney used diesel oil to provide the fuel because when diesel fuel burns, it creates little smoke. Too much smoke would have obscured the actors.

Ron wanted the flames to creep across the ceilings of rooms—a feat not easily accomplished. After all, fire is unpredictable. Hall and Pinney found it was much easier to make the fire creep along the floor, so to deliver what Ron requested they simply constructed some of the sets upside down—making the floors into the ceilings.

Of course, the actors had to be protected from the flames. During the fire scenes, the actors and stunt workers wore flame-retardant suits similar to the garments worn by race car drivers who often find themselves in fiery crashes. The suits won't protect the wearers from heat and flames for long—just a minute of so—but that's usually long enough for help to arrive. Still, there were close calls and accidents.

Ron said:

> We started filming before we had run all those tests, without knowing everything we could do. It was the most frightened I've ever been making a movie. We came so close to having some serious accidents on the movie. One time I cued a mortar at the wrong time and almost burned Kurt Russell. At another time, some barrels blew up that weren't supposed to at a certain time; gratefully, nobody was around. One of our actual firefighters who was acting in the movie had his eyebrows singed off. When he got home, his wife flipped out. She said, 'In 10 years on the department you've never been hurt and now you've gotten burned on a stupid movie. What's going on?' We were consciously pushing the envelope but trying desperately not to get anybody hurt.

To film the fire scenes, the cameras had to be protected from the heat as well. So the special effects experts developed shields for the photography and sound equipment made out of the same ceramic tiles that protect the Space Shuttle as it hurtles into the atmosphere during re-entry from space. Without those tiles, the Shuttle would burn up from the incredible heat caused by the friction of the atmosphere against the fast-moving spacecraft.

The title of the movie refers to a situation familiar to firemen. A fire burns silently in a closed-off room, using up most of the oxygen in the enclosed area. When an unknowing victim opens the door, suddenly introducing a source of fuel to the fire, the blaze erupts in a tremendous fireball, blasting out from the room and burning anyone and anything in its way. That phenomenon is known as a "backdraft."

What Howard was able to accomplish in the movie was to create the notion that the fire, itself, was a character—the true villain of the story. Hall and Pinney were able to show the fire creeping silently toward victims as though it were a living, breathing killer.

"I became involved with *Backdraft* because I was fascinated with the idea of trying to deal with fire as kind of a character. A lot of the actors . . . who came on board said I wish I could play the fire because it was written so vividly in the script," said Howard. "It was one of the great attractions of the movie."

Indeed, the characters in the movie speak of the fire not as the spontaneous combustion of heat, friction and fuel, but as an equal. "Don't let it know you're scared," Stephen hisses at Brian, as the two brothers make their way up the stairs of a burning building.

In one scene, Robert DeNiro, who portrays an arson investigator, tells Brian: "It's a living thing, Brian. It breathes. It eats. And it hates. The only way to beat it is to think like it."

Playing the role of a former arsonist called upon to help solve the mystery of a rash of unexplained fires, seasoned actor Donald Sutherland brought his experience and talent to *Backdraft*.

And when Brian visits a jailed arsonist played by Donald Sutherland to learn more about the unknown arsonist setting backdraft fires around the city, Sutherland's character tells him: "Whoever did this knows the animal well. They know him real well, but they won't let him loose. They won't let him have fun, so they don't love him. Now, who doesn't love fire?"

The answer, as Brian soon learns, is a Chicago fireman

setting the fires to kill conspirators who have been robbing the city's fire department budget that, the arsonist believes, has been causing the deaths of firemen.

Critics embraced the film. Janet Maslin of *The New York Times* wrote: "The spectacular fire sequences, which must have been hellish to film, are powerfully enveloping on screen."

And David Denby, film critic for *New York* magazine, said, "This is what the big screen and special effects are *for.* Ron Howard, the director, treats fire as a living thing. It breathes, hides, roars defiance. A monster with a malign spirit and nasty tricks, it comes rushing through an open door like a tidal wave. And there's an eerie element, a mystic brotherhood of flame: Fire talks to certain people. It talks to spooky Donald Sutherland, quite unnerving as a pathological torcher, and to Robert DeNiro, an obsessed arson expert. Some of the special effects are predictable: Beams fall; ceiling collapse; canisters explode. But the flames, billowing and beckoning, infinitely sinister, almost talk to us as well."

Audiences embraced the film, too. *Backdraft* earned $150 million at the box office. Pinney won an Academy Award for special effects—one of three awarded to the film for technical achievements.

"It's just astounding the work these special effects guys did," said Widen, the screenwriter. "I wouldn't say this movie was a documentary, but I do think it comes the closest anyone has ever come to what it's like to be in there and to move around inside" a building on fire.

The film *Far and Away* starred Tom Cruise and Nicole Kidman as Irish immigrants seeking their fortune in nineteenth-century America. Despite Ron's hard work and attention to period details, the film scored modestly at the box office.

Chapter 6

Great Storytelling

FOLLOWING THE CRITICAL acclaim and audience acceptance of *Backdraft,* Howard's next project was *Far and Away,* an ambitious film that told the story of Irish immigration to America and the opening of the nation's western frontier. The story took place in the 1880s, and painstakingly created the hardscrabble plight of immigrants. What's more, Howard cast film stars Tom Cruise and Nicole Kidman in the lead roles of Joseph and Shannon. With such talent on both sides of the camera, the film should have been a major box office success. But critics panned the film and audiences stayed away.

Critics applauded Howard for the look of the film, pointing out that the movie accurately captured the sooty atmosphere of crowded cities near the end of the 19th century as well as the colorful spirit of pioneers in America, but they complained that the story was shallow and predictable. Writing in the *Chicago Sun-Times,* critic Roger Ebert said the movie "joins astonishing visual splendor with a story so simple-minded it seems intended for adolescents." *Far and Away,* which cost $50 million to make, barely recorded a profit.

Howard said:

> If I have a regret about *Far and Away* it's that I feel a little bit robbed . . . The experience was just darn near perfect, and then the critics absolutely nailed us. It was so disheartening because [it was] this thing that had been kind of a magical two-year filmmaking experience, a realization of a kind of a dream to make a certain kind of a film. At every preview screening we had it generated great applause and terrific reaction and the critics hit us hard. I did feel it was kind of tainted. . . . I always felt kind of cheated because it was the realization of a long-time dream.

If Ron thought the critics were hard on *Far Away,* his next project was likely to undergo the most intense media scrutiny of his career. In Ron Howard's 1994 movie *The Paper,* the character of city editor Henry Hackett is portrayed by Michael Keaton. It is Hackett's job to head a staff of dozens of reporters for the fictional *New York Sun*—a tabloid newspaper with a thirst for news of murders, train derailments, celebrity scandals, and crooked politicians.

Hackett's wife Martha is played by Marisa Tomei. In the film, Martha is pregnant and just days from her due date. Nevertheless, Henry never seems to have time for

Ron's film *The Paper* centers on 24 hours in the life of a fictional New York tabloid newspaper. Here, Ron directs Michael Keaton, who plays the paper's editor and who starred in Ron's earlier film *Night Shift*.

her—he is constantly called away by the demands of his newspaper.

When Henry breaks a date with Martha for dinner because he has to help a reporter obtain information from a reluctant source, she angrily confronts him. She says, "Let me give you a hypothetical. A guy with a gun breaks into the house and holds it to my head. He says, 'Either I blow your wife's brains out or I blow up the *Sun* building. Choose. Now.' What do you say?"

"Don't take the bat out of my hand," Henry answers. "This is the ninth inning—you know what it's like. I got to get the quote. This guy isn't going to be there all night."

He then runs off to interview the source.

Pete Hamill loved that scene. Hamill has spent most of his adult life working in tabloid journalism as a reporter, columnist and editor. For *The Paper,* he served as a technical advisor to the filmmakers and even appeared in the movie in a cameo role.

As for the scene between Henry and Martha, Hamill said, "In my time I've known dozens of newspaper people who've had to make less melodramatic versions of that choice. Even today, when decent wages have allowed them to adopt the guise of suburban respectability, reporters and editors, male or female, are often faced with the same dilemma. They always choose the newspaper."

Nonetheless, Ron nervously awaited the reviews. Film critics are, after all, news reporters, and most of them work for newspapers. They know all about how newspapers run, and they are loathe to permit Hollywood license to glamorize the profession of journalism.

"I figured I was kind of walking into a propeller," Howard said. "I assumed there was no way we could get it 100 percent right. I remember realizing at one point that I've never seen a film about filmmaking that rang 100 percent true to me. No way we're going to get this 100 percent right about the journalists. They were probably going to nail us."

But they didn't. The feared newspaper critics found a lot about *The Paper* to praise. Just as he had done with *Backdraft,* Howard devoted considerable time studying tabloid newspapers, spending weeks hanging around reporters and editors at New York's two competing tabloids —the Post and Daily News.

Hamill was recruited to guide the filmmakers through the world of tabloid journalism.

"Howard and his collaborators impressed me with the seriousness of their method," said Hamill. "Like good

In *The Paper*, actress Glenn Close played the Sun's managing editor, Alicia Clark. The film's intensity and character development earned Ron the respect of his peers.

reporters, they were not trying to impose preconceived notions on the scene before them; they were soaking up facts and allowing those facts to shape the story. That's why I was convinced that they wanted to make a good movie about newspapers, an accomplishment that has been oddly rare. In most newspaper movies, reporters and editors are either boneheads or swine."

There is no question, though, that some movies about the newspaper business are regarded as classics in American filmmaking. The 1931 movie *The Front Page* is a hilarious comedy about unscrupulous reporters outwitting crooked and bumbling politicians while covering an execution. In 1952, movie icon Humphrey Bogart played an editor of a dying newspaper named *The Day* who manages to use the last edition of the paper to uncover the crimes of a local mobster. In the final scene of the movie, Bogart speaks by phone with the hoodlum from the newspaper's pressroom; when the presses start rolling to produce the last edition of paper, the hoodlum asks Bogart the source of all the racket.

"That's the press, baby," Bogart says. "The press! And there's nothing you can do about it—nothing!"

In 1976, Robert Redford and Dustin Hoffman played relentless reporters Bob Woodward and Carl Bernstein in the film version of *All the President's Men,* the story of how *The Washington Post* brought down the corrupt administration of President Richard M. Nixon.

In Howard's movie, the *New York Sun* is a city tabloid—a style of newspaper that became familiar to American readers in the 1920s. Unlike a "broadsheet" newspaper, a tabloid doesn't have to be unfolded to be read: it is smaller than a broadsheet and opens like a book—ideal for the subway commuter, who doesn't have much elbow room to spread open a broadsheet on a crowded train.

The city tabloids go after a different type of news than readers are used to seeing in the broadsheets. Readers looking for news about Congress, the White House, or the governor's mansion would do well to look in the broadsheets. Crime always makes the headlines in the tabloids, as do fires, train wrecks, and similar catastrophes. Tabloids love scandal—particularly if it involves a local politician or civic leader.

Tabloid readers are also sports fans and, indeed, they are given a large dose of sports news in their papers.

Tabloid editors use a lot of photographs—known as "art" in the language of the journalist—because they know their readers respond to pictures as much as words. In fact, some of the earliest tabloids were known specifically as picture newspapers. For years, the *New York Daily News* proclaimed itself as "New York's Picture Newspaper," and it still includes a tiny drawing of a camera in its flag, which is the newspaper's name in bold type displayed on the front page. In *The Paper, Sun* managing editor Alicia Clark, played by Glenn Close, argues that the newspaper should feature a subway derailment as its lead story. "People got maimed, and we got pictures of it," she points out.

On every page, tabloid readers will find bold headlines written to capture the readers' attention and hold it. In Ron's movie, when editors kick around some ideas for a headline, one of them says, "God forgive this paper ever run a headline without an exclamation point."

The Paper centers on 24 hours in the life of the *Sun*. The film begins with the *Sun* getting beat by the competing tabloids on a big story—the murders of two visiting businessmen. While the Sun has led its front page with a story about the New York City parking commissioner getting caught parking illegally, the other papers are all over the murders. "Welcome to New York—You're Dead" screams the headline in the *New York Daily News*. Hackett resolves to get a follow-up on the murders, and for the next 24 hours he drives his reporters to dig up an exclusive while battling other editors to commit the newspaper's resources to the story. Along the way, Ron shows the newsroom of the *Sun* as a pulsating place of incandescent excitement where reporters and editors shout at each other, joke with each other, get in each other's way and, somehow, manage to produce a daily newspaper under deadline. "Coal into a furnace, Henry," says *Sun* editor Bernie White, played by Robert Duvall. "I've been doing this for 36 years—every day you start with zero."

In *The Paper*, Ron did a great job of recreating the high-pressure world of a sensationalist New York tabloid. Here, the paper's staff meets to choose their next cover story.

Film critic John Powers at *New York* magazine was impressed with the ability of Howard and screenwriters David and Stephen Koepp to recreate a tabloid newsroom. He said the "script shows off their feel for daily-paper bedlam: [air-conditioning] repairmen clogging the aisles between cubicles, headline writers with their 10,000 small questions, sniffy editors whining about second-hand smoke, prima donna columnists who swagger even when lying down. In love with the kick-ass lingo of tabloid life, the Koepps can't get enough of Henry yakking with five people at once (and) editors swapping bitchy remarks at the morning story meeting."

In the film, the *Sun* prevails. Henry's reporters dig out

the exclusive he wants—the two young black kids arrested for the murder are innocent, and the businessmen are really victims of a mob hit. Henry wins the tangle with his boss, who agrees to stop the presses so the updated story can run in the next day's paper. Henry and Martha's baby is born. In fact, Howard splices footage from the hospital delivery scene with film of the *Sun's* huge metal presses, folders and bundling machines spitting out copies of the paper.

"This story of 24 hours in a newspaper's life doesn't say that any job worth doing is doing well," wrote Richard Alleva, film critic of the magazine *Commonweal.* "It says that big city success depends upon beating your opposition. And if beating out your rivals means that you must teeter on the edge of a nervous breakdown for sixteen hours a day, six days a week—all the better! Only squares and dopes want to live ulcer-free lives."

If Howard received a measure of personal fulfillment for *Far Away* and critical acclaim for *The Paper,* his next project would earn him the respect of his peers.

Apollo 13 became Howard's most ambitious film—his studio granted him a budget of $65 million to recreate the ill-fated mission to the moon. It was a lot of money, to be sure, inasmuch as films about the American space program had largely been failures.

In fact, there had been few movies about America's real-life astronauts although, certainly, there has never been any question about their heroism, the danger of their missions or the importance of the significant discoveries they have made in space. Certainly, audiences have always been in love with movies about space—but the successful films have usually been science-fiction stories with no basis in reality.

In 1983, director Philip Kaufman tried to break the mold

with the film version of *The Right Stuff,* author Tom Wolfe's book about the early days of the American space program. Although Kaufman was given high marks for remaining accurate to the true exploits of America's original astronauts, audiences were hardly impressed and the film bombed at the box office. It seemed as though Americans were much more interested in the fictional adventures of Luke Skywalker and Han Solo in *Star Wars* than in the real-life stories of John Glenn and Chuck Yeager.

"I almost chickened out on *Apollo 13,*" Howard recalled. "It was pretty expensive. At the time, you know, $60 million or $62 million, it was still pretty high-end. *The Right Stuff* was a great movie that lost the studio a lot of money. Tom Hanks was really interested in doing *Apollo 13,* but every time I would talk about casting Hanks, friends would say, 'Oh, is it a comedy about space?'"

At the time, Hanks had not yet made his mark as a dramatic actor in *Philadelphia* and *Forrest Gump,* and was still regarded mostly as the star of screwball comedies, such as *Bachelor Party* and *Volunteers.*

"Tom was incredibly articulate and passionate about the subject, and I thought he would be a good collaborator," said Ron. "Two things kept buoying me. One was that every time I read the script, I would get emotional. And that's rare. And then the other thing was that—and this is really kind of telling—other directors I respected were really sniffing around."

Indeed, as Howard launched himself into the project, it soon became clear in the moviemaking world that *Apollo 13* would be one of the major studio releases of 1995.

Even so, there was one nagging question hanging over the production: How would audiences respond to the retelling of a story in which the outcome was already

Ron cast Tom Hanks (center), Bill Paxton, and Kevin Bacon as the crew of *Apollo 13*. Although Hanks had been known as a comic actor, the role gave him a chance to excel at a dramatic role.

known? The result of the mission was well recorded in the history books—Lovell, Haise, and Swigert returned safely to earth. Would Howard be able to keep movie viewers on their edges of their seats while the capsule limped home from the moon, even though everyone in the audience knew all three astronauts would survive?

"Story is king," Ron explained. "The greater achievement of *Apollo 13* was not the technological stuff. It was in developing a flow to the story through which we were able to blend the three environments of home, Mission Control and the capsule in a way that allowed the sequences to build and communicate the danger, the sacrifice, the courage and the emotional stress that these people were feeling without resorting to situations where the characters would be saying things they would never say in real life."

The secret, he said, was to present the story in human terms—to show the personal battles fought by the astronauts, their families and the flight controllers at Mission Control during the flight. He wanted to make the audience feel their fear, pain, and bravery. Ron explains:

> My attitude about *Apollo 13* changed from the time I committed to making it to the time that we actually began filming it. In the beginning, I approached it for the same reason I approached *Backdraft*—this was a great cinematic challenge; I could use today's technology to really allow the audience to feel what it must be like to be in a spacecraft. I had no idea how we'd do it, but that's a great challenge. I am a proponent of the space program, it would be interesting to kind of salute the space program. But then as I started doing the research, and particularly one day when I went to the actual Mission Control room, and met with a bunch of Mission Control veterans, I started to understand what the experience was like—not only for the astronauts, but the people on the ground. It was life or death for them in a very, very personal way and unlike kind of a war situation—it was much more like a battlefield medical unit. These mission controllers had a huge personal investment in not losing the patient. I began to understand the whole movie in much more personal and heroic terms.

Ron Howard won the 1995 Outstanding Feature Film Directorial Achievement Award for his work on *Apollo 13*. The award is presented by the Directors Guild of America, the association of film directors. The film directors themselves vote on the DGA Award, meaning that the recipient has earned the highest regard of his peers. He missed out that year on the Academy Award for Best Director, but Ron still valued the DGA Award because it meant that his fellow professionals had now recognized him as the best.

Said Tom Hanks: "The achievement on *Apollo 13* was that he had limited scope and a story that everyone knew the ending of, and he had to find some way to make it human and understandable and gripping. That he did it as well as he did, that's a reason he won the DGA Award that year. It really is great storytelling."

In creating a film version of the Dr. Seuss cartoon "How the Grinch Stole Christmas," Ron harnessed the comic energy of Jim Carrey to create a film that would appeal to audiences young and old.

Chapter 7

This is the Grinch

RON FOLLOWED *APOLLO 13* with *Ransom,* the story of a kidnapping gone wrong, and *EDtv,* a satirical look at an instant celebrity invented by a cable television show. *Ransom* was a bona fide Howard hit, garnering $162 million at the box office, but *EDtv* bombed badly, earning just $23 million—far below the $60 million the studio spent to produce the film.

A major reason *EDtv* failed to fill theaters is that it told essentially the same story that audiences had seen the year before in *The Truman Show.* In *EDtv,* a video store clerk named Ed allows a camera crew to follow him around 24 hours a day, broadcasting his life on a popular cable television program. In *The Truman Show,* an insurance salesman named Truman Burbank is followed around by TV cameras recording his life, but Truman remains oblivious to this fact for much of the film.

EDtv starred Matthew McConaughey, a dedicated and accomplished actor with many film credits. *The Truman Show* starred Jim Carrey, an internationally-known comedian famous for his physical, face-contorting comedy. Is it any wonder that *EDtv* was upstaged by *The Truman Show?*

"Of course, I would have preferred to be the first of these films out but I refused to rush *EDtv,*" Howard said. "I considered scuttling the film except that I felt we were different enough that it shouldn't matter."

Clearly, audiences didn't see it that way. Still, as a filmmaker Ron had always been able to learn from his mistakes. For his next project, the live-action production of Dr. Seuss' *How the Grinch Stole Christmas,* Howard selected the one actor he believed could bring the right amount of comic energy to the role of the Grinch: Jim Carrey.

Theodor Seuss Geisel's first book was titled *And to Think That I Saw It on Mulberry Street.* It was rejected by 43 publishers before he convinced a friend to finance its publication. The book went on to moderate success, but eventually Geisel, who wrote and illustrated under the name Dr. Seuss, became the world's most successful author of children's literature.

What young reader has never heard of Horton the Elephant, Daisy-Head Mayzie, the Sneetches, or Bartholomew Cubbins? How many of his readers have wondered about the taste of green eggs and ham? Before Geisel, most children learned to read by paging through the adventures of Dick and Jane, two fictitious children who

Generations have enjoyed Dr. Seuss' famous Christmas character the Grinch. In directing the film version, Ron used his talents as a director to bring "Whoville" to life. Here, the Grinch holds dog Max and Little Cindy Lou Who in the original Dr. Seuss drawing.

led rather ordinary lives. In 1954, *Life* magazine published a stinging criticism of children's literature, claiming that kids were bored with Dick and Jane and that's why they were having trouble learning how to read. Geisel's publisher, Bennett Cerf, saw the *Life* magazine article and challenged Geisel to craft a beginning reader's book that would teach the use of the most fundamental words while still being fun to read. In fact, Cerf sent Geisel a list of 250 words for the book that new readers might be learning. In 1957, Geisel met Cerf's challenge, and produced *The Cat in the Hat.*

That year, Geisel also published another book: *How the Grinch Stole Christmas.* It told the story of the green-skinned Grinch, who was born with a heart "two sizes too small," living in a cave atop a mountain overlooking the village of Who-ville. As Christmas approaches, the cranky Grinch conjures up the "wonderful awful" idea to ruin Christmas for the Whos. Accompanied by his sidekick, a dog named Max, the Grinch dons a Santa outfit and spends Christmas eve traipsing from home to home, stealing gifts, Christmas trees, decorations, and holiday food. At the end of the story, the Grinch watches as the Whos gather to sing Christmas carols and realizes that Christmas is about much more than presents, wreaths, and treats.

> And what happened then . . . ?
> Well in Who-ville they say
> That the Grinch's small heart
> Grew three sizes that day!

Geisel's young fans were certainly familiar with the story. Many of his older fans even recalled the 1966 animated television special based on the book that featured the narration of Boris Karloff, the veteran horror actor.

The TV special spanned a mere 30 minutes, which Howard believed was hardly enough time to fully explore the comic potential of the story and, in particular, the character of the Grinch.

"I kept saying, 'Why is he in a cave? Why is he living with a dog? What's going on? What's that all about?'" Ron said. "Many of my favorite scenes are scenes where he is alone in the cave, just tied in knots, figuring out what he's going to do next. Simply put, I decided that how the Grinch stole Christmas would be the third act, and the first two acts would be why the Grinch stole Christmas, and we would work with it comically and work backward from the clues that we had and develop some other ideas."

There was no question, though, that to make the audience believe in the Grinch, Carrey had to become the Grinch on the screen. And to transform Carrey into the Grinch, Howard called on the considerable talents of Rick Baker.

When Rick Baker was growing up in Binghampton, New York, he would save his nickels and dimes to buy copies of the magazine *Famous Monsters of Filmland.* Inside, Baker found grainy black-and-white photographs of ghouls, zombies, and vampires created by Hollywood makeup artists. In the late 1950s and early 1960s, when Baker was a young boy, the studios producing horror films released such titles as *I was a Teenage Frankenstein, The Fly,* and *Invasion of the Body Snatchers*—low-budget productions that relied on the ability of the makeup artists to make monsters that were believable and frightening to the audience. There was very little technology involved; the artists used putty, greasepaint, and glue to make a monster.

While many of his friends had dreams of becoming baseball players or firemen, Baker decided at a young age to become a Hollywood makeup artist. Indeed, when Baker was 10 years old, he was already using his talent to paint fake bruises, gashes, and even gunshot wounds onto his friends.

"I liked people to believe the makeup I did was real," Baker said. "There was one guy I made up with this horrible burn. He went home, and his father was hysterical."

When he was 20 years old and majoring in art in

Make-up artists Rick Baker and Gail Ryan accept the Academy Award for their work in *The Grinch*. Bringing the cartoon figure to life was one of the great challenges and joys of Baker's career.

college, Baker was hired to create makeup for a low-budget film that was being directed by a student filmmaker named John Landis. The film was titled *Schlock* and featured an ape-like monster named the Schlockthropus that was played by Landis. The film won some awards and Landis eventually became a successful Hollywood director. Baker, meanwhile, became a busy and innovative makeup artist, finding work on such films as *The Exorcist, Live and Let Die,* and the 1976 remake of *King Kong.* When Landis and Baker joined forces again in 1981 for Landis's film *An American Werewolf in London,* the collaboration proved to be a stunning achievement for Baker. His work on *American Werewolf* won the first Academy Award given out for the category of Best Makeup.

Over the next two decades, Rick Baker became Hollywood's most sought-after makeup artist. His work revolutionized the craft. During his career, he worked on some of the most successful movies in history, applying makeup to the industry's major stars.

So, when Ron needed someone to bring the Grinch to life, he knew just whom to call. Baker may have learned his craft by painting scars and bruises on his 10-year-old friends in Binghampton, but virtually every technique employed by Baker as well as other Hollywood makeup artists can be traced to an actor who shot to fame during the era of the silent cinema. In 1913, Lon Chaney was a struggling actor surviving on small roles he found on Carl Laemmle's Universal Pictures studio lot. In those days, if the director needed a pirate for a scene, he would summon a group of actors and select someone for the job whom he thought resembled a pirate. After attending several such "cattle calls," Chaney started bringing a makeup kit with him; if the director wanted a pirate, Chaney would make himself up as a pirate on the spot, winning the role and, more importantly, a day's pay. Between 1913 and 1918 Chaney appeared in more than 100 such roles, earning him the status as the "Man of a Thousand Faces."

Chaney soon reached stardom, owing to his talent as an actor as well as his desire to take on challenging, often physically demanding roles. For his role as Quasimodo in *The Hunchback of Notre Dame,* Chaney strapped a 50-pound hump and harness to his back, purposely twisting his spine so that he could experience the pain he believed the tragic figure of the bell ringer endured in the classic Victor Hugo novel.

A similar experience awaited Jim Carrey as he prepared to play the Grinch. Rick Baker and his assistants spent months designing the Grinch makeup, which was far more sophisticated than the stage makeup that Chaney applied to his own face to make himself look like a hideous pirate or a scary ghoul. The face and body of the Grinch was sculpted out of foam rubber that would be glued onto Carrey's skin in layers. For inspiration, Baker looked over Geisel's drawings of the Grinch, but since Geisel had illustrated the Grinch with basically pen-and-ink drawings, the artists working on Howard's movie had to find ways of making the Grinch look three-dimensional on the screen.

Baker and his assistants worked on several designs. At one point, when they believed they were close to the final version, Baker had the makeup applied to himself. Photographs and videotapes of Baker wearing the Grinch "appliance" were sent to Howard and Grazer, who weren't satisfied. They wanted the Grinch to look like the Grinch but also be recognizable as Jim Carrey. Finally, Baker decided that Carrey had to brought in for the final fittings.

"Jim really wanted to go with a minimal approach to begin with, so we tried a very small appliance on him, a little brow cover thing," said Baker. "I didn't think it was

In creating a Grinch that would be recognizable to audiences as actor Jim Carrey, make-up artist Rick Baker took a lesson from classic films like *The Hunchback of Notre Dame*. In this classic shot, the hunchback is played by actor Lon Chaney, who made the role famous.

enough. To make a long story short, we went through at least half a dozen tests. It kept coming back to 'just paint him green because he can make this cool Grinch expression.' I was heartbroken."

During one of the makeup sessions, Carrey saw the photographs of Baker that had been sent to Howard and Grazer. Baker said, "Jim got up to take a break. He says, 'What's this? This is what the Grinch should look like. This is the Grinch.' My jaw just kind of dropped. I was glad to hear him say that. I said, 'I agree, this is what I feel the Grinch should be. But everybody's had different ideas. You said a few seconds before that you wanted to be painted green.' He said, 'I'll go for it, if I can look like this.' So I showed him the video of me in the Grinch makeup and he got more excited about it."

The movie moved on to the production stage. Prior to each day's shooting, Carrey had to sit in a makeup chair for some three hours while Baker and his assistants transformed him into the Grinch. To keep the star's spirits high during 90 days of incessantly boring makeup sessions, Howard hired standup comedians to perform private shows for Carrey.

Tedious makeup sessions were the least of Carrey's problems during the filming. The layers of foam rubber and yak feathers composing the Grinch makeup were incredibly uncomfortable and hot; to make things bearable for Carrey, Howard had the air-conditioning on the movie set cranked up to full blast. Also, the makeup proved painful—Carrey was forced to wear false yellow eye lenses over his real eyes. At one point, the pain became too much for the actor to endure and he ripped the rubber mask and false eyes from his face.

"It was tough the first couple of weeks," Carrey said. "It was impossible to scratch my nose. Every once in a while I'd punch myself in the leg or pinch my arm to take the focus off my discomfort."

Howard found a way to coax his star through the discomfort. He hired a Navy SEAL to teach Carrey mind-control techniques for enduring pain and stress. SEALs are Navy commandos trained to enter the most dangerous combat situations; they are able to reach deep within themselves to overcome danger, fear, and pain to accomplish their missions.

Both devilish and loveable, Jim Carrey's performance as the Grinch helped make Ron's film a holiday hit.

Clearly, the finished film reflected Jim Carrey's dedication to the role, Rick Baker's genius as a makeup artist and Ron Howard's talent as a director. The film became Howard's most successful movie, earning $260 million at the box office. It is one of the 20 most profitable movies ever produced in Hollywood. And Rick Baker won an Academy Award for creating the Grinch.

Critics embraced the film as well. Writing in *People Weekly,* critic Leah Rozen said, "Carrey brings antic zest to his part but also locates the Grinch's brusied heart." *Maclean's* magazine critic Cheryl Hawkes said that while she watched the film, "the 10-year-old in the next seat whispered, 'Jim Carrey was never better!'" And writing in *Commonweal* magazine, critic Rand Richards Cooper said, "Carrey transforms Seuss's brooding curmudgeon into a high-octane standup comic."

By the time *Grinch* hit the theaters Howard had established himself as one of Hollywood's most successful directors. Since the first few dollars had rolled in on *Grand Theft Auto,* Howard's films had earned nearly $1 billion in box office receipts. Most of those movies were produced in partnership with Brian Grazer; together, the two men formed Imagine Entertainment, a Hollywood production company that not only generates theatrical film releases, but has also spawned the HBO miniseries *From the Earth to the Moon* as well as situation comedies, including *Sports Night* and *Felicity.*

Away from Hollywood, Howard has settled into an idyllic life in Connecticut, where Ron and Cheryl elected to raise their four children—Bryce, Jocylyn, Paige, and Reed—far from the glitter of the movie industry. The Howards have taken pains to raise their children in as normal an environment as possible, just as Rance and Jean Howard made it clear that the shooting schedule for *The Andy Griffith Show* would not interfere with their son's Little League games.

Following his work on *Grinch* Howard's next project was *A Beautiful Mind,* the story of John Forbes Nash Jr., a Nobel Prize-winning mathematician who was afflicted with the mental illness schizophrenia. Academy Award-winning actor Russell Crowe starred in the role of Nash.

Another project Howard pursued was *The Burial,* a film that follows the life of Willie Gary, an African-American lawyer practicing in Mississippi who battles racism while representing a local funeral home owner in court against a large morturary conglomerate. And Howard also has hopes of directing a remake of *The Alamo,* which was originally

Ron's latest film, *A Beautiful Mind*, stars Russell Crowe as a mathematical genius struggling with his own demons. The film is based on a true story and has proven another big hit for Howard at the box office.

released in 1960 with John Wayne in the role of Davy Crockett, one of the leaders of the Texans who made an ill-fated stand against Mexican invaders in 1836.

Said Howard: "I hope that people who enjoy movies will simply think that a film of mine is worth giving a chance to—that it stands an above-average chance of being good, involving, and worthy of their 90 to 120 minutes. I hope that it can reach a point where they don't try to categorize it as comedy or action-drama, a thriller or a fantasy. Hopefully, they'll say, 'Ron Howard directed it, that's probably worth checking out.' To me, that would be very satisfying."

1954 Ron Howard born in Duncan, Oklahoma on March 1

1956 Plays first stage role in *The Seven Year Itch*

1959 Appears in first film role as Billy Rhinelander in *The Journey*

1960 Stars as Opie Taylor in the long-running TV show *The Andy Griffith Show*

1969 Wins second place in an amateur filmmaking contest sponsored by Kodak for his film titled *Deed of Derring-Do*

1973 Stars in the film *American Graffiti*

1974 Plays Richie Cunningham in the hit TV show *Happy Days*

1975 Marries Cheryl Alley

1977 Directs his first film, a low-budget production titled *Grand Theft Auto*

1978 Directs *Cotton Candy,* a made-for-TV teen romance

1980 Meets producer Brian Grazer and they form a partnership that eventually becomes the production company Imagine Entertainment

1981 *Night Shift,* Ron's first mainstream theatrical film, is released

1984 His second film, *Splash,* earns $109 million at the box office and establishes him as one of Hollywood's hottest directors

1985 Directs *Cocoon,* another box office success

1988 His film *Willow* features dazzling special effects but is a critical and box office bomb

1989 The film *Parenthood* reestablishes him as a hot director, earning $132 million at the box office; the comedy examines the problems faced by young parents in America

1991 Directs the film *Backdraft,* which scores an Academy Award for special effects and other technical achievements

1995   *Apollo 13* becomes a huge critical and commercial success, earning more than $172 million at the box office and garnering him the Outstanding Feature Film Directorial Achievement Award from the Directors Guild of America

2000   *How the Grinch Stole Christmas* is released; the film wins an Academy Award for Best Makeup

2001   Directs *A Beautiful Mind*

2002   Wins Best Director and Best Picture Academy Awards for *A Beautiful Mind*

1977   *Grand Theft Auto*

1978   *Cotton Candy* (TV)

1980   *Skyward*

1981   *Through the Magic Pyramid* (TV)

1982   *Night Shift*

1984   *Splash*

1985   *Cocoon*
       No Greater Gift (TV)

1986   *Gung Ho*

1987   *Take Five* (TV)

1988   *Willow*

1989   *Parenthood*

1991   *Backdraft*

1992   *Far and Away*

1994   *The Paper*

1995   *Apollo 13*

1996   *Ransom*

1999   *EDtv*

2000   *Dr. Seuss' How the Grinch Stole Christmas*

2001   *A Beautiful Mind*

Alleva, Richard. "The Paper and Proxy." *Commonweal,* May 20, 1994.

Armstrong, Lois. "Happy Days are Here Forever as Ron Howard Plays Cecil B. in the Big D." *People Weekly,* June 12, 1978.

Beck, Ken, and Clark, Jim. *The Andy Griffith Show Book.* New York: St. Martin's Press, 1985.

Birnbach, Lisa. "The Man Who Makes 'Normal' Trendy." *Parade,* April 7, 1985.

Burman, John. "Film Directors Hollywood Can Bank On." *Bergen County Record,* Nov. 24, 2000.

Cagle, Jess. "Faces: For Monsters, Monkeys or Five Eddie Murphys, Who You Gonna Call? Rick Baker." *Time,* July 31, 2000.

Castro, Peter. "Ron Howard: Child Labor." *People Weekly,* July 24, 1989.

Cieply, Michael. "Opie-Wan Howard Visits Fantasy World in 'Willow.'" *Los Angeles Times,* Jan. 17, 1988.

Cooper, Rand Richards. "Home for the Holidays: 'How the Grinch Stole Christmas' and 'Two Family House.'" *Commonweal,* Dec. 15, 2000.

Corliss, Richard. "Everybody Into the Pool." *Time,* June 24, 1985.

Corliss, Richard. "Hell of a Ride." *Time,* July 3, 1995.

Corman, Roger, and Jerome, Jim. *How I Made a Hundred Movies in Hollywood and Never Lost a Dime.* New York: Random House, 1990.

Denby, David. "Lord of the Earrings." *New York,* June 3, 1991.

Ebert, Roger. "Far and Away." *Chicago Sun-Times,* May 22, 1992.

Farber, Stephen. "Ron Howard Goes From Hot Actor to Hot Director." *The New York Times,* June 16, 1985.

Fierman, Daniel. "Get Happy." *Entertainment Weekly,* April 16, 1999.

Fink, Mitchell. "False Alarm." *People Weekly,* June 10, 1991.

Goldner, Diane. "Real-Life Firefighters Heat up 'Backdraft.'" *People Weekly,* June 17, 1991.

Gronemeyer, Andrea. *Film—An Illustrated Historical Overview.* Hauppauge, New York: Barron's Educational Series, 1998.

Hamill, Pete. "A Media Event." *New York,* March 21, 1994.

Harrison, Nancy. "For a Baldwin Brother, Star Billing is a Switch." *The New York Times,* Aug. 4, 1991.

Hawkes, Cheryl. "Spectacular Seuss." *Maclean's,* Nov. 27, 2000.

Hobson, Louis B. "With *EDtv,* Director Ron Howard Explores the Price of Fame—Is It Any Wonder?" *Calgary Sun,* March 21, 1999.

Horn, John. "The Filmmaker Series: Ron Howard." *Premiere,* April 1999.

Howard, Ron. "Sticker Shock Hits Hollywood." *U.S. News and World Report,* Jan. 1, 1996.

Johnson, Brian D. "Fear of Frying." *Maclean's,* June 3, 1991.

Johnson, Malcom. "Rick Baker is the Man Behind the Grinch's Green Guise." *The Hartford Courant,* Nov. 23, 2000.

Kael, Pauline. "The Current Cinema." *The New Yorker,* Aug. 15, 1985.

Kahn, Sheryl. "Fathers Know Best." *McCall's,* August 1996.

Kalbacker, Warren. "Playboy Interview: Ron Howard." *Playboy,* May 1994.

Kauffman, Stanley. "Poor Richard's Almanack, and Others." *The New Republic,* July 15- 22, 1985.

Kauffman, Stanley. "Types." *The New Republic,* June 17, 1991.

Kihn, Martin. "Simulating the Times." *New York,* March 21, 1994.

Kligman, David. "Live on RONtv." *Entertainment Today,* April 2-April 8, 1999.

Kluger, Jeffrey. *The Apollo Adventure.* New York: Pocket Books, 1995.

Leonard, Sheldon. *And the Show Goes On.* New York: Limelight Editions, 1995.

MacFarquhar, Larissa. "The Producer." *The New Yorker,* Oct. 15, 2001.

Marshall, Garry. *Wake Me When it's Funny.* Holbrook, Massachusetts: Adams Publishing, 1995.

Maslin, Janet. "'Backdraft,' Firefighting Spectacular." *The New York Times,* May 24, 1991.

Maslin, Janet. "Screen: 'Cocoon' Opens." *The New York Times,* June 21, 1985.

Mast, Gerald, and Kawin, Bruce F. *A Short History of the Movies.* Needham Heights, Massachusetts: Allyn and Bacon, 2000.

Maychick, Diana. "Ron Howard Makes Another Splash." *Mademoiselle,*
   July 1985.

Novak, Ralph. "Screen: Backdraft.*" People Weekly,* June 3, 1991.

O'Toole, Lawrence. "When the Old Become New." *MacLean's,*
   July 1, 1985.

Powers, John. "The Paper," *New York,* March 21, 1994.

Rafferty, Terrence. "Getting the Story." *The New Yorker,* March 28, 1994.

Ressner, Jeffrey. "Nice Guy at Mission Control." *Time,* July 3, 1995.

Rozen, Leah. "Dr. Seuss' How the Grinch Stole Christmas."
   People Weekly, Nov. 27, 2000.

Sampey, Kathleen. "Ron Howard's Career More Like King's 'Ransom.'"
   The Associated Press, Nov. 22, 1996.

Sanders, Richard, and Hutchings, David. "In the Sleeper of the Summer
   Cocoon's Don Ameche Catches Hollywood's Younger Sex Symbols
   Napping." *People Weekly,* Sept. 2, 1985.

Schmidt, William. "Chicago Goes for the Burn in the Making of
   'Backdraft.'" *The New York Times,* Jan. 20, 1991.

Scott, Elaine. *Movie Magic: Behind the Scenes with Special Effects.*
   New York: Morrow Junior Books, 1995.

Dr. Seuss. *How the Grinch Stole Christmas.* New York: Random
   House, 1957.

Taylor, Al, and Roy, Sue. *Making a Monster: The Creation of Screen
   Chracters by the Great Makeup Artists.* New York: Crown
   Publishers Inc., 1980.

Taylor, Chris, and Ressner, Jeffrey. "Tinseltown Titans Caught in
   a Web." *Time,* Sept. 18, 2000.

Weinraub, Ron. "The Dark Underbelly of Ron Howard." *The New York
   Times,* Nov . 12, 1996.

Welkos, Robert W. "Right Guy for the Gig?" *Newsday,* Nov. 19, 2000.

Werts, Diane. "TV's Child Stars Grapple with Grown-Up Woes."
   Newsday, July 6, 2001.

Young, Tracy. "Invasion of the Hollywood Offspring." *Vogue,*
   June 1985.

Weidt, Maryann N. *Oh, the Places He Went: A Story About Dr. Seuss.*
   Minneapolis, Minn.: Carolhoda Books, 1994.

Winkler, Henry. *The Other Side of Henry Winkler.* New York: Warner Books, 1976.

Zucchino, David, and Hotz, Robert Lee. "New York Firemen Hold on to a Very Hard Hope." *Los Angeles Times,* Sept. 12, 2001.

"The Directors: Ron Howard." Videocassette, directed by Robert J. Emery. Media Entertainment Inc. and the American Film Institute, 1997.

"Hollywood Takes Wing as Cocoon Takes Off in the Theaters." *People Weekly,* July 8, 1985.

"Kid Actors Like Trained Animals: Howard." The Associated Press, Nov. 6, 1996.

"Real Fire Fails to Stir 'Backdraft' Audience." The Associated Press, Aug. 11, 1991.

"Ron Howard Movie Company Loses by Default in Script Lawsuit." The Associated Press, June 6, 1996.

Box Office Report
[http://boxofficereport.com/media/profiles/howard.shtml]

Changing the Way the World Sees the Elderly
[http://www.seniorworld.com/articles/a19991014113031.html]

Desson Howe's *Parenthood* Review
[http://ofcs.rottentomatoes.com]

Directors Guild of America
[http://www.dga.org/news/mag_archives/v21-2/howard.html]

Dr. Seuss
[http://www.seuss.org/seuss/seuss.bio.html]

Edtv
[http://www.cpcn.com/articles/032599/20q.shtml]

F/X Great Rick Baker Dishes on Grinch, Apes Remake
[http://mrshowbiz.go.com/]

George Lucas: The Creative Impulse
[http://www.cwrl.utexas.edu/~daniel/309m/project4/christal/lucas.html]

Hollywood Meets NASA in *Apollo 13*
http://www.cnn.com/SHOWBIZ/Movies/Apollo13/]

Jim Carrey warms up to another mask
[http://www0.mercurycenter.com/justgo/special/grinch/interview-carrey.htm]

KC-135 Zero Gravity Trainer
[http://zea.lerc.nasa.gov/kjenks/kc-135.htm]

Lon Chaney
[http://www.lonchaney.com/lc5/sr/srpages/srbiok.html]

Lon Chaney
[http://www.cinemaweb.com/silentfilm/chaney/]

Lon Chaney: Man of a Thousand Nightmares
[http://www.mdle.com/ClassicFilms/FeaturedStar/star8a.htm]

The Mighty Rick Baker
[http://members.tripod.com/candles-2/id139.htm]

McGill Researchers Solve Mystery of Space Sickness
[http://exn.ca/Stories/1997/08/22/03.asp]

Motion Pictures Related to Aging
   [http://www.aging.ufl.edu/apadiv20/cinema.htm]

New York Fire Department Losses at World Trade Center
   [http://www.americanfirejournal.com/magazine_articles.htm]

Rick Baker's Academy Awards Acceptance Speech
   [http://www.oscar.com/oscarnight/winners/makeup.html]

Roger Ebert's Review of *Willow*
   [http://ofcs.rottentomatoes.com]

Ron Howard's Who-ville Owes Its Look to Sources Ranging From Frank
   Lloyd Wright to *Citizen Kane*
   [http://www0.mercurycenter.com/justgo/special/grinch/interview-howard.htm]

Space Motion Sickness
   [http://ccf.arc.nasa.gov/dx/basket/factsheets/sms.html]

Beck, Ken, and Clark, Jim. *The Andy Griffith Show Book.* New York: St. Martin's Press, 1985.

Corman, Roger, and Jerome, Jim. *How I Made a Hundred Movies in Hollywood and Never Lost a Dime.* New York: Random House, 1990.

Gronemeyer, Andrea. *Film— An Illustrated Historical Overview.* Hauppauge, New York: Barron's Educational Series, 1998.

Kluger, Jeffrey. *The Apollo Adventure.* New York: Pocket Books, 1995.

Leonard, Sheldon. *And the Show Goes On.* New York: Limelight Editions, 1995.

Marshall, Garry. *Wake Me When it's Funny.* Holbrook, Massachusetts: Adams Publishing, 1995.

Mast, Gerald, and Kawin, Bruce F. *A Short History of the Movies.* Needham Heights, Massachusetts: Allyn and Bacon, 2000.

Scott, Elaine. Movie Magic: *Behind the Scenes with Special Effects.* New York: Morrow Junior Books, 1995.

Dr. Seuss. *How the Grinch Stole Christmas.* New York: Random House, 1957.

Taylor, Al, and Roy, Sue. *Making a Monster: The Creation of Screen Chracters by the Great Makeup Artists.* New York: Crown Publishers Inc., 1980.

Weidt, Maryann N. *Oh, the Places He Went: A Story About Dr. Seuss.* Minneapolis, Minn.: Carolhoda Books, 1994.

Winkler, Henry. *The Other Side of Henry Winkler.* New York: Warner Books, 1976.

About the author

Hal Marcovitz is a journalist for *The Morning Call,* a newspaper based in Allentown, Pennsylvania. He has written more than 30 books for young readers, including biographies of actor Robin Williams and civil rights activist Al Sharpton. He lives in Chalfont, Pennsylvania, with his wife Gail and daughters Ashley and Michelle.